CHORD THEORY: FOR BEGINNERS

2 Manuscripts in 1 Book, Including: Music Theory and How to Play Chords

Preston Hoffman

Table of Contents

MUSIC THEORY
FOR BEGINNERS
The Only 7 Exercises You Need to Learn
Music Fundamentals and the Elements
of Written Music Today
PRESTON HOFFMAN

BOOK 1

MUSIC THEORY: FOR BEGINNERS

The Only 7 Exercises You Need to Learn Music Fundamentals and the Elements of Written Music Today

Preston Hoffman

Table of Contents

Introduction

Thank you and congratulations on purchasing this book, *"Music Theory: For Beginners"* I have written this book to provide you with the steps that you need to take to understand the fundamentals of music theory from a beginner's standpoint.

One of the most common problems that many people face when it comes to music theory is the inability to get a good book that sticks to the fundamental aspects. Music theory is not exactly a topic that will get your heart pounding, so most people want content that will explain music fundamentals in a clear and concise manner. Most music theory books either bore the reader with long, drawn-out explanations, or they toss in some complex concepts that leave you totally confused.

However, this is where this book is different. This book provides you with the only seven exercises that you need as a beginner to master the fundamental elements of written music. These interactive exercises are all based on seven topics that form the basis of every good music theory course. The exercises are spread throughout the book so that once you finish reading each chapter, you can test yourself. I have taken the time to make the questions as challenging as possible yet simple enough for any beginner to understand. In any case, the answers have been provided at the end of the book.

You will not find yourself struggling with complex theories here. I have written this book with the beginner in mind, so every chapter covers a single aspect of music theory. This is to ensure that you move step-by-step, mastering one foundational topic before you move onto the next one. You will learn the common notation system, scales, clefs, key signatures, intervals, chords, and much more.

I have tried to make sure that the topics move sequentially in terms of the level of difficulty. My goal is to take your hand and walk you through every topic and exercise so that you feel comfortable with the content. From my experience with reading and writing music, I know that if you get the first step right, then the next one will automatically fall into place.

By the time you finish reading this book, you will be much more confident in reading and even writing your own music. Yes, it's true! The exercises you will go through in this book will test you and help you grow your musical abilities. I can promise you that with this book, you will finally get to learn all you ever wanted to know about music theory in a fun and interactive way. This is a personal guarantee!

Are you ready? Let's go!

Chapter One: Understanding Music Theory

In this chapter, you will learn about what music theory is all about and why it is important for beginners to have a firm theoretical foundation. You will also go through a brief and painless history of written music. Finally, you will get to discover the seven exercises that are fundamental to the learning of music.

What is Music Theory?

The simplest way to define music theory is this: It is the language that enables you to read, understand, and play any kind of music that has been composed. Music theory is made up of rules and concepts that are designed to govern the way music is written and performed.

Another way to look at it is that music is a language that consists of many various parts. Each part is then divided into smaller sections. If you want to learn how to speak the whole language, you must start by learning the smaller sections first and how to combine them to form the larger parts. Then you must learn how to put together those large parts to communicate whatever message you have through that language.

We learn music theory so that we know how to put the elements together to compose music. That is music theory in a nutshell.

As a beginner, it is easy to fall into the trap of feeling overwhelmed when you hear the words "music theory," but there is really nothing to worry about. The critical thing to keep in mind when learning about music theory is that the music preceded the theory. The art of making musical sounds dates back thousands of years, and at that time, our ancestors didn't have any kind of theory to rely on. They just pounded on their drums and played it by ear. If you are already playing an instrument, then you most likely have a rough idea about music theory. The only issue is that you haven't learned the terms and technicalities yet.

Like I said before, music theory is a language that allows musicians to read and perform compositions the way the composer intended. However, it is important to also note that there are some musicians who are not able to read or write music, yet they can still make awesome melodies and sounds. There are some people who can hear and speak English but cannot read or write it. Therefore, some people view learning music theory as boring and unnecessary.

On the other hand, I believe that a student can progress much further in learning a new language by training himself/herself to read and write it. It is the same with music theory. If you want to master new techniques, gain more confidence, and perform new styles, you need to learn music theory.

Now let's go back a bit into history to unearth the beginnings of music theory.

Musical Beginnings

According to historians, complex musical instruments were already being used as far back as 7000 B.C. Archaeologists have found bone flutes that can still be used to create short performances for modern listeners to hear.

There are pictographs from 3500 B.C. that depict the ancient Egyptians playing clarinets, harps, and lyres. By the year 1500 B.C., the people in Northern Syria had modified the Egyptian harp and created the first ever two-stringed guitar. The instrument even had tuning pegs and a hollow soundboard for amplifying sounds.

So why am I telling you all this?

If you look at the history of ancient music, you will realize that distinct cultures spread out all over the world were able to create music with very similar tonal qualities. How was this possible? It is believed that certain patterns of musical notes just sound right while others do not. If this is the case, then music theory is simply the search for why and how certain notes sound right or wrong. To put it more plainly, music theory is important because it helps us understand *why* an object sounds a particular way and *how* we can reproduce that exact sound.

Ancient Greece is believed to be the origin of music theory. The Greeks even built schools that taught the science and philosophy of analysing music. It was Pythagoras who went as far as creating the 12-pitch octave scale that resembles the one we currently use today. Pythagoras achieved this using a device known as the Circle of Fifths, which you will learn about later in this book.

A lot of the musical theory you are about to learn is based on the works of the ancient Greeks. But unlike the Greek language, this book is much simpler to read and understand.

The Significance of Theory in Your Music

It is easy to think that making great music is as simple as sitting down, playing whatever note you want, going in any direction you see fit, and even stopping at any stage of the performance. That is often the view of most aspiring musicians who would love to play an instrument.

However, such kind of performances, if they do exist, would cause confusion and sound annoying to the listeners. Only those musicians who have thoroughly mastered how to stack notes and chords adjacent to each other can manage to perform a spontaneous jam that listeners would love. In other words, since music is a language that communicates a message, you must learn how to connect with your listeners at all times.

Learning musical theory can also inspire you a great deal, as you will soon find out after you finish reading this book. It is a tremendously great feeling when you discover that you can put together a chord progression and create an awesome song out of it. How would you feel if you could look at a piece of classical music and know that you can play it for the first time?

What about being confident enough to call up your friends and ask them to come over and jam with you? You wouldn't be able to do that without learning music theory since you need a way to communicate with other musicians. You use music theory to talk to one another as you play your various instruments.

The truth is that music theory will broaden your horizons as a musician. If you see yourself as a potential rock guitarist, you will be able to know which notes to play in which key. If it's classical music you are interested in, you will know how to sight-read and maintain a consistent beat. Music is fun but it also requires a prominent level of discipline. At the end of it all, it is worth it!

The Seven Fundamental Exercises

There are a lot of elements that you will have to learn to become an accomplished musician. Of course, we all wish that we could somehow sit down with an instrument and start playing beautiful music without going through the hassle of any formal training. But the reality is that you need structured exercises that will prepare you for your future as a music maestro.

In the next few chapters, we are going to cover music theory fundamentals that will help you get started. There are seven elements that you will have to master to learn these elements effectively. They are:

1. Learning the staff and music alphabet

2. Common notation

3. Basic elements of music (rhythm, melody, harmony, etc)

4. Mastering the scales

5. Building intervals

6. Understanding key signatures

7. Forming chords

Every single one of these elements is critical to your progress as a beginner. They will teach you the individual elements of music and how they are put together to create a solid foundation for reading, playing, and studying music.

Chapter Summary

Here is a summary of the key points of this chapter:

- Music theory is the rules and concepts that enable us to read, understand, and play any kind of musical composition.
- It is possible to play music without learning music theory, but if you want to go further in learning new techniques and performing new styles, you must learn music theory.
- Though complex musical instruments date back as far as 7000 B.C., the ancient Greeks are the ones credited with establishing schools for analysing the elements of music.
- Learning musical theory will enable you to communicate more effectively with listeners and fellow musicians, while also inspiring confidence in your own musical abilities.
- There are seven key exercises that will help you learn the fundamentals of music theory.

In the next chapter, you will learn about the staff and how we use the music alphabet to write music. It isn't a difficult topic, but since the rest of the book will be based on what you learn in the next chapter, you need to make sure that you go through it thoroughly.

Chapter Two: Learning the Staff

In this chapter, you will learn about the staff. It is important to start by learning the main way that we write music. You will learn what the staff looks like, the several types of clefs, and how to arrange notes when writing your music. There will also an exercise at the end of the chapter to test what you have learned.

Human beings started making music way before writing was invented. Even to this day, some musicians choose to play "by ear," which means they don't rely on written music. However, it is important to write music so that it can be shared and studied. This means that we must have system to represent music, hence the need for a music alphabet.

What is the Music Alphabet?

The musical alphabet is an arrangement of letters that enables us to write the sounds that we want to play. Every time you sit down to play music with others, the first thing you do is talk about what you plan on playing. By talking I don't mean just telling each other stories or describing your music verbally. The language of communication should be specific to music, and that is where the music alphabet comes in. The alphabet is the means of representing your music.

Before we go into the musical notes themselves, let's start by learning about the most widespread way of writing music. This is the staff.

The Staff

Now that you have learned about the music alphabet, it's time to tackle a very important component of music. All instruments that play specific pitches are written on the staff, which is comprised of five horizontal parallel lines. Music notes are usually placed either on the lines or in the spaces between the lines. The music on a staff is read from left to right.

In the image below, you will notice some short lines that are above or below the staff. These are known as *ledger lines*. These are used to show a note that is too low or too high to be placed on the staff.

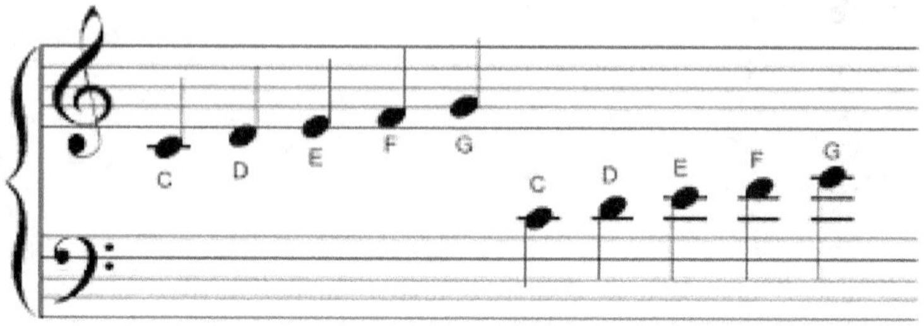

Figure 2.1

To make reading music much easier, vertical lines are used to split the staff into sections. These lines are known as **bar lines**. Each section that is formed on the staff is then called a *measure* or **bar**. At the end of every staff, there are two lines that mark the end of a section of music or song. These are known as **double bar lines**. A heavy double bar line indicates that you have reached the end of the song. A light double bar line means the end of a section of music.

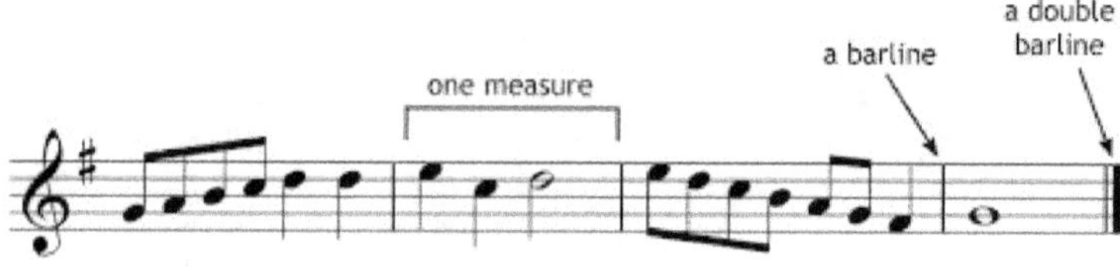

Figure 2.2

You may be wondering what some of the symbols and shapes are on the staff above. These will be discussed later in this chapter.

Clefs

In figure 2.2, you notice a symbol that is placed at the beginning of the staff. This is the *Clef symbol*. It tells you the type of note that is found on every line and space of the staff. There are two kinds of clefs; the treble clef (or G clef) and the bass clef (or F clef).

The reason why it's called a G clef is that its body curls around the line that represents the G note. For the F clef, the symbol curls around the line representing the F note. The notes in the staff are always arranged in ascending order from top to bottom, but they are positioned differently depending on the type of clef being used. The reason why we use different clefs is to cover as many notes within the human voice range as possible, as well as most of the instruments used. People and instruments with high voice ranges use the treble clef while those with lower ranges use bass clef.

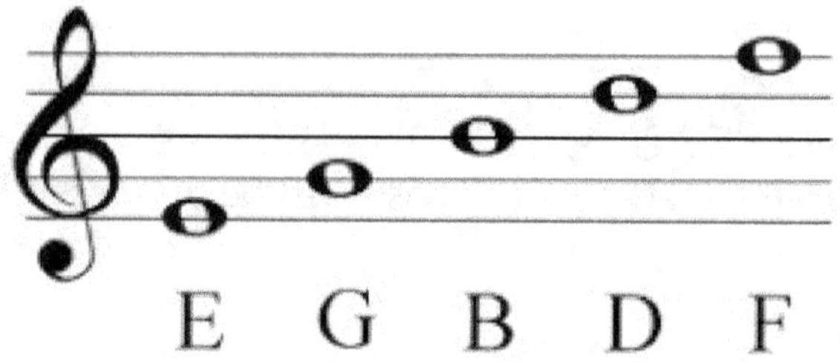

Figure 2.3

Figure 2.4

Exercise 1

1. Draw the staff on a piece of paper and practice writing the two clef symbols on the staff. Draw as many as you can until you learn it perfectly.

2. Draw the staff with treble and name all the spaces on the staff.

3. Draw the staff with bass clef and name the lines in it.

4. On a staff with a treble clef, name the ledger lines and spaces above the staff.

5. On a staff with a bass clef, name the lines and spaces below the staff.

Chapter Summary

Here are some key points you need to remember:

- The musical alphabet is an arrangement of letters that enable us to write the sounds that we want to play.
- The notes on the staff are placed either on the lines or in the spaces between the lines.
- Notes on the staff are arranged in ascending order.
- Ledger lines are used when showing notes that are too high or too low to appear on the staff.
- A bar line splits the staff into sections called measures or bars.
- A heavy double bar line indicates the end of a song.
- A light double bar line indicates the end of a section of music.

- There are two types of clef symbols – the treble clef and the bass clef.

In the next chapter, you will learn about music notation. These are considered the building blocks of music and are necessary when writing your music.

Chapter Three: Understanding Common Notation

In this chapter, you will learn the A-B-C's of the musical language. We will talk about the building blocks that form the foundation of musical theory. These include notes, pitch, octave, beats, and time signature. There will also an exercise at the end of the chapter to test what you have learned.

Common notation simply refers to the standard system that we use to represent music notes. It is more widely used than other types of music notation that have been invented, for example, tablature. You have already learned about one part of common notation in the previous chapter. Now let's talk about notes and pitches.

Notes

Every piece of music you will encounter consists of notes. They are the building blocks of music. A note is simply a letter of the musical alphabet that represents the *pitch* made by a musical instrument.

The pitch of a note refers to how low or high it sounds. Pitch is dependent on the frequency and wavelength of the sound wave of a note. If the frequency of the sound wave is high, and the wavelength is short, the pitch will be high. Since very few musicians are keen on such kind of physics terminologies, they use letters to represent different pitches.

There are seven letters that form the music alphabet. These are:

A B C D E F G A

or:

C D E F G A B C

These seven letters are used to name the white keys on a keyboard. As you can see above, you start with the letter A and proceed to the letter G. After G, instead of going to H, we go back and start counting from A. In music, each set of seven letters (A – G or C - B) is referred to as an **octave**. The moment you reach the eighth note, you begin the next octave.

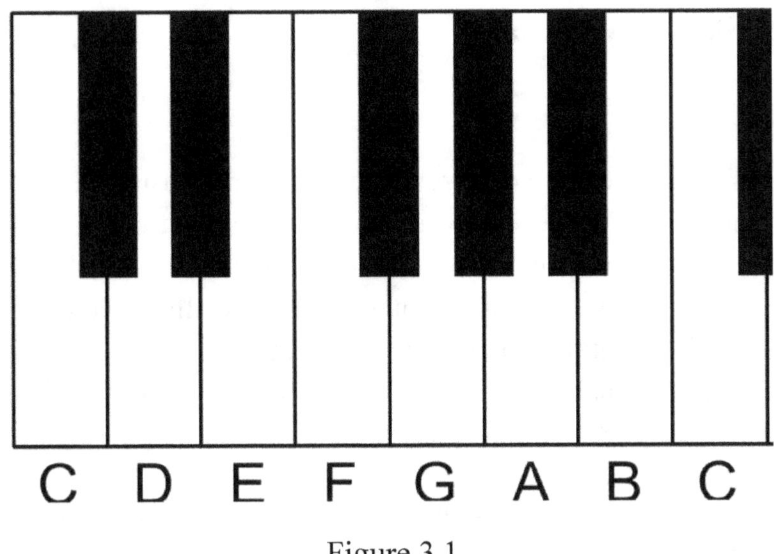

Figure 3.1

But there's one thing that you need to be keenly aware of here. As you move toward the right side, or *up the alphabet*, you realize that you will meet a note with the same letter name as another one before. However, this next note will be at a higher octave than the previous one.

In figure 3.1 above, the second C note has a pitch that is at a higher octave than the first. If you were to move up the alphabet, the third C note would be a higher pitch than the second one, and so on. You can also move in the opposite direction, and this is referred to as going *down the alphabet*.

Sharps and Flats

Though there are only seven letters in the music alphabet, there are more than seven notes. The seven letters from A to G represent *natural* notes. Natural simply means it is a regular note. However, there are five other notes that are usually placed in-between these natural notes. This brings the total number of notes in the music alphabet to 12. These five other notes are represented as *sharp notes* (♯) and *flat notes* (♭).

A sharp note is a note that is higher in pitch than its natural letter. For example, G♯ (pronounced G sharp) is higher than G. On the other hand, a flat note is a note lower than its natural letter, so A♭ (pronounced A flat) is lower in pitch than A. These sharp and flat notes are used to represent the black keys on a keyboard.

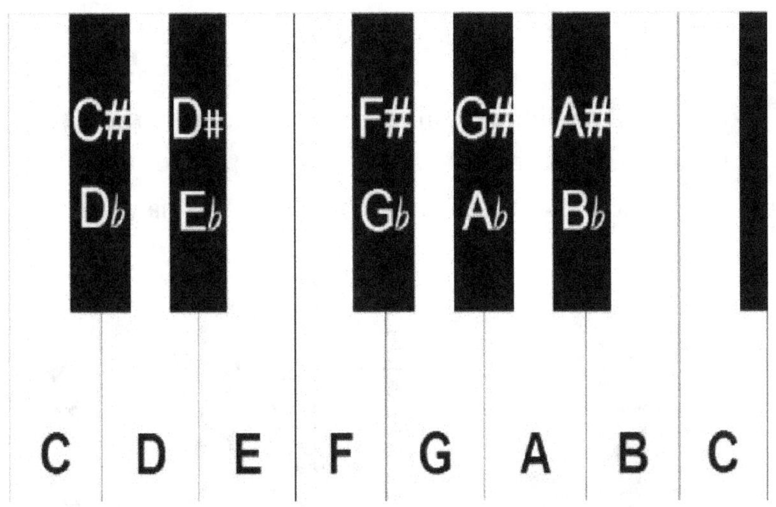

Figure 3.2

From the image above, you can see that in some instances, the sharps and flats occupy the same key. This means that they refer to the same note but are given different names depending on where they are used. This is what is known as ***enharmonics***. In other words, F♯ is the same note as G♭, and C♯ is the same note as D♭, and so on.

If you are keen, you may have noticed that there are some notes that do not have any sharps or flats between them. This happens between the E-F notes and B-C notes. This shouldn't be taken to mean that there is no E♯ or C♭. We simply refer to them as F or B. So, when you raise an E by one note you get an F. Also, when you lower a C note you get a B.

The sharp symbol usually indicates that the particular note is one half-step higher than its natural equivalent. For example, G♯ is one half-step higher than G. In the same way, the flat symbol indicates that the note is one half-step lower than its natural equivalent. So, A♭ is one half-step lower than A.

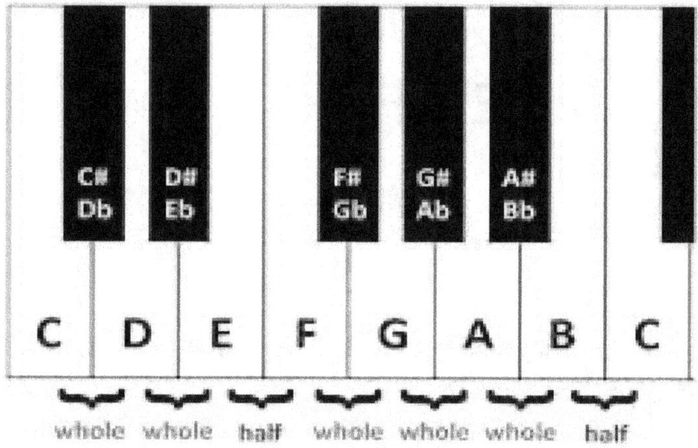

Figure 3.3

In other words, the distance between the G note and the A note is *one whole step*. When you see two adjacent notes having a sharp or a flat note between them, then that means that they are a whole step apart. Therefore, from figure 3.3, it is clear to see that most of the notes on the keyboard are one whole step apart except the E-F notes and B-C notes. These are only one half-step apart.

Parts of a Note

In common notation, sounds are written in form of notes. The two most critical pieces of information that written music should convey to a musician are the pitch to be played and its duration. A note that is placed high on the staff should be played at a higher sound.

To determine the pitch of a note, look at the clef, key signature, and the line or space the note is placed. To determine the duration of a note (how long it lasts), you look at the shape of the note, its tempo, and time signature.

There are three specific parts of a note. There is the head, the stem, and the flag.

- **The Head** (3) – This is the rounded section of a note. The head can be shaded or hollow. Every note must have a head.

- **The Stem** (2) – This is the vertical straight line that is linked to the head. Quavers, crotchets and minims all contain stems. Stems can point either up or down depending on the position of the note on the staff. Notes on or above the centre line have stems pointing down. Notes below the centre line have stems pointing up.

- **The Flag** (1) – This is the line that sticks out from the top or bottom of the stem. Only quavers and shorter notes carry flags.

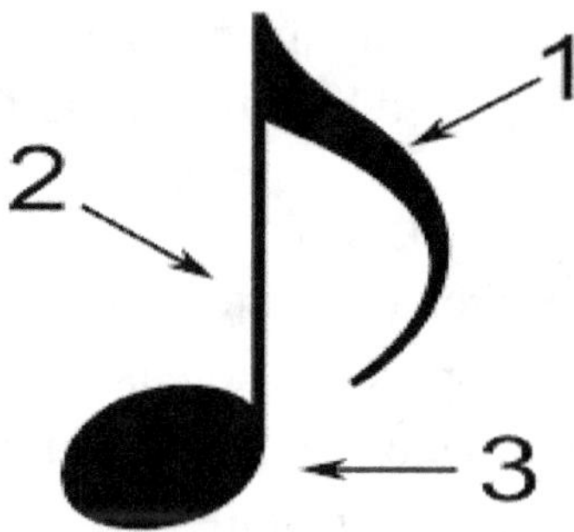

Figure 3.4

The pitch of a note is determined by the position of the head of the note, not the entire body. The head, the stem and the flag are all factors that must be considered when deciding how much time a note is given.

Note Duration and Values

Note duration is defined as the amount of time that a note is played. Each note usually has its own value, and these include the semibreve, minim, crotchet, quaver, and semiquaver. They are shown in this exact order in the image below.

Figure 3.5

The Whole (Semibreve) Note

This note is represented by a hollow oval and has no stem. It is the longest note in modern music and lasts for a full four beats.

31

This means that for four entire beats, all you must do is play and hold that one note.

The Half (Minim) Note

This is half the value of a semibreve and is held for half as long as the whole note. Two minims occupy the same length of time as a semibreve. It is represented by a hollow oval with a stem.

The Quarter (Crotchet) Note

This is a quarter of a semibreve. Four crotchets occupy the same length of time as a semibreve, which means a crotchet is one beat long. It is represented by a shaded oval with a stem.

The Eighth (Quaver) Note

This is half the length of time as a crotchet. It is represented by a shaded oval with a stem and a flag. The flag cuts the value of a note by half.

The Sixteenth (Semiquaver) Note

Two semiquavers occupy the same length of time as one quaver. It is represented by a shaded oval with a stem and two flags.

If two notes that have flags are next to each other, they are sometimes connected using a **beam**. This makes it possible to group flagged notes so that the music is easier and faster to read. The same principle also applies to semiquavers. A note must have the same number of beams as it does flags.

Figure 3.6: Semiquaver with beam

Dotted Notes

By now you know that a minim is half the length of a semibreve; a crotchet is half of a minim, and so on. But what do you do if you want a note length that is not half of another note? That's where the dotted note comes in. A dotted note is 1 ½ times the length of the same note. So, you end up with the original note length and half of that note length. For example, a dotted minim would have a duration that is as long as a minim plus a crotchet; or three crotchets.

If a note has two dots, it simply means that each dot adds half the length of the previous note. This is shown in figure 3.7 below.

Figure 3.7

Time Signatures

These are usually indicated at the front end of the staff and are placed after the clef symbol and key signature. The time signature doesn't appear on every staff. It is used only when there is a change in the meter. *Meter* refers to the basic rhythm of the music. Time signature represents the meter and tells you how you should write it.

A fraction represents time signatures. The number at the top indicates the number of beats per measure while the number at the bottom indicates the type of note that will be used to carry the beat. The next section explains this more clearly.

Figure 3.7

Beats

There are many ways to organize music, and one of them is by splitting the time into small periods known as **beats**. Most of the actions that go with a piece of music occur at the start of the beat. For example, when you tap your foot or clap your hands, you are making those sounds or movements at the start of the beat. This is usually referred to as being "on the downbeat" since it corresponds to the moment when the conductor's baton reaches the bottom of its path.

The downbeat is the most substantial section of a beat, though some are stronger than the rest. Beats form a pattern such as strong-weak-weak-strong-weak-weak. Therefore, beats are further grouped into measures or bars. For example, a beat such as strong-weak-weak-strong-weak-weak would be written as 1-2-3-1-2-3, which means that each measure must contain three beats.

We already talked about how time signature indicates the number of beats per measure and the kind of note that carries a beat. For example, figure 3.7 has a time signature that requires three quarter (crotchet) notes in all the measures on that particular staff. In other words, every measure will have three crotchets. We usually say that such a piece is in "three four" time.

Don't forget what we learned earlier. A crotchet (quarter) note is one beat long. In other words, every measure on the staff should have the equivalent of three beats. These can still be represented as one minim and a crotchet, or six quavers per measure.

Exercise 2

1. Complete the following series of natural notes: A B
   _ _ E F _ _

2. Provide an alternative name for the following:

   a. A♯

   b. D♭

   c. G♭

   d. E♭

Fill in the blanks:

3. 1 semibreve = _____________ quavers

4. 1 minim = _____________ quarters

5. 1 minim = 1 quarter + _____________ eighths

6. Draw two staves with a treble clef symbol and time
    signatures showing *two four-time, three eight time,*
    and *six four time*. Fill in each measure with a
    different combination of note lengths. Use at least
    one dotted note in each staff.

Chapter Summary

Here are some of the key points you need to remember:

- A note is a letter that represents the pitch made by a musical instrument.
- An octave is a set of notes from one letter to the next pitch by the same letter name.
- The symbol ♯ represents sharp notes.
- Flat notes are represented by the symbol♭.
- Enharmonics are two notes that have equal pitches but are known by different names.
- There are five note values - semibreve, minim, quarter, quaver, and semiquaver. Each note lasts half the beat of the previous one.
- Music is divided into short time periods called beats.
- The time signature is shown using a fraction. The number at the top indicates the number of beats per measure. The number at the bottom indicates the type of note that will be used to carry the beat.

In the next chapter, you will learn about the building blocks of music. These are the basic elements of every musical piece, and they include aspects like rhythm, harmony, melody, timbre, and dynamics.

Chapter Four: The Basic Elements Music

In this chapter, you will learn about the essential elements that make music what it really is. These are aspects that even non-musicians can understand. As long as you have an appreciation for good music, you should be able to pick out these musical building blocks.

We are going to cover a number of these basic elements here. It is also important to note that musical theory experts hold differing opinions as to the total number of the elements of music. Some claim that there are as few as four while others say that there are as many as 10. Here we shall be covering rhythm, harmony, melody, timbre, texture, and dynamics.

Creating Rhythm

The primary reason why we study music theory is to be able to describe different musical pieces regarding how similar or different they are about the above six elements. Rhythm is considered one of the most basic components of any kind of music. Some types of music don't have harmony or melody, but every piece of music must have rhythm.

So, what exactly is rhythm?

Rhythm can be defined as the pattern of sounds repeated throughout the music. We can also say that rhythm is the arrangement of note lengths in music. Music and time go hand in hand, which means that rhythm has to be heard over a period of time. Rhythm is usually shaped by the meter and incorporates other elements such as *tempo* and *beat*.

Tempo is the speed at which you play a particular piece of music. When creating a composition, you indicate the tempo using an Italian word. For example, if you look at the starting point of a score, you may see words like *Largo* (slow pace), *Moderato* (moderate pace), or *Presto* (very fast pace). Here are some common tempo markings and their translations:

- Adagio – slow

- Vivo – lively and brisk

- Lento – slow

- Molto – a lot

- Mosso – motion or movement

- Piu – more

- Allegro – fast

- (un) poco – a little

- Meno – less

Harmony

Harmony is the result of having more than one pitch being heard at the same time. When you hear two or more notes being played at one time, you are listening to harmony. Harmony provides support for the melody and gives it texture. Harmony is usually described as being diminished, augmented, major, and minor.

Melody

Melody can be described as the general tune that is created when you play a succession of notes. It is influenced by your rhythm and pitch. A musical piece can have just one melody running through it, or it may have several melodies stacked in a verse-chorus form.

Timbre

Timbre is the quality of a sound that differentiates one musical instrument or voice from another. It is also called *tone color*. Timbre has nothing to do with the volume, length, or pitch of a sound.

For example, if you play a specific note on a clarinet and then on an oboe for five seconds at a specific volume, a listener can easily know that the notes are different. This is because the timbre of a clarinet is different from that of an oboe.

Texture

This refers to the type and number of layers that are used in a musical composition. Texture can be a single melodic line (monophonic), several melodic lines (polyphonic), or the main melody together with chords (homophonic).

Dynamics

This is the intensity that a musical piece is performed. In written music, dynamics are represented by symbols or abbreviations that indicate the volume that a note should be sung or played. Just like tempo, dynamics are derived from Italian words. For example, *fortissimo* indicates an extremely loud passage while *pianissimo* indicates an extremely soft section of music.

Here are some typical dynamic markings:

- mf mezzo forte   = medium loud

- f   forte   = loud

- ff fortissimo   = very loud

- fff fortississimo   = very, very loud

- p   piano   = soft

- pp pianissimo   = very soft

- mp mezzo piano   = medium soft

Exercise 3

1. Test yourself and see whether you can interpret what
   these Italian tempo markings mean:

   - Poco pin mosso

   - Piu vivo

   - Un poco allegro

   - Molto adagio

2. Write these dynamics in order from the quietest to
   the loudest: f, p, mf, ff, pp, and mp

Chapter Summary

Here are some of the key points you need to remember:

- Rhythm is the pattern of sounds repeated throughout the music.
- Rhythm depends on the tempo and beat of the music
- Tempo refers to the pace of the music and is usually indicated by Italian words.
- Harmony is created when more than one pitch is played at the same time.
- Melody is the general tune created when a succession of notes is played. A musical piece can have one or more melodies.
- Timbre is what tells us the difference between sounds made by different instruments.
- Texture is the number and type of layers in a musical composition. It can be monophonic, polyphonic, or homophonic.
- Dynamics is the intensity that music is played, and its markings are derived from Italian words.

In the next chapter, you will learn more about the different types of music scales. These are considered to be subsets of the notes you learned in Chapter 3.

Chapter Five: Forming Music Scales

In this chapter, you will learn how to create the different types of music scales. You will start with the simplest one, which is the major scale, and then proceed onto the more complex minor scale.

Music scales can be described as a set of notes arranged in sequential order, chosen to be used for a particular song. Why do we choose those notes? Simply because they sound great together! Though different cultures have adopted a variety of scales, the most common one is the major scale.

In order to create a scale, you need to go through the music alphabet (remember the seven letters from A to G?) and pick out notes that go well together. The notes chosen must achieve a particular sound. In most cases, you can do this by combining whole steps and half steps.

Tonal Centre

Every scale begins with the note that it is named after. That particular note is referred to as the *tonal centre* of that scale, and it is where the music in that scale feels "at rest."

For example, in most cases, music in the C major scale always ends on a C major chord. The music will begin on the C note, return to the C note repeatedly, and the melody will be based on the C note so much that listeners be able to identify where the tonal centre of that piece of music is.

Major Scales

If you have ever heard a song that sounds cheerful, uplifting, and fun, then it was probably written in a major key. Music that is written using a particular key only uses some of the many notes available. This sequence of notes then forms what we call a scale. Major keys are used to build major chords to then form a major scale.

It is important to know that different songs can use different scales, and different parts of a song can also make use of different scales. Scales are normally written in a sequential order from one note to the next note of the same letter. For example, we can have a scale that ranges from note C to the next note C, as shown below.

C D E F G A B C

As we already learned, each set of seven letters of the music alphabet forms an octave. Therefore, we can say that the above scale is a one-octave scale. To create a two-octave scale, you simply continue the same sequence until you land on the next note with the same letter name.

C D E F G A B C D E F G A B C

The range of notes from C to C is what forms the scale for C major. None of the notes in this particular scale has a sharp or a flat. On the other hand, the D major scale has two sharps. These are F sharp and C sharp.

D E F♯ G A B C♯ D

So, the question you are probably asking is: How are we supposed to know which notes should be sharpened and which ones should be flattened? The first method involves the use of a chart. However, this can be a cumbersome way since you have to keep referring all the time. You may even be forced to cram all that information into your head. The better alternative is to learn how to use whole and half steps.

Whole Steps and Half Steps

We talked about how the pitch of a sound represents how high or low the sound is. In music, we usually say that one note is either much higher or lower than another. This distance between two pitches is known as a half step. If you look at figure 5.1 below, you will be able to understand this better. This method of counting up whole and half steps can be used to form music scales from scratch.

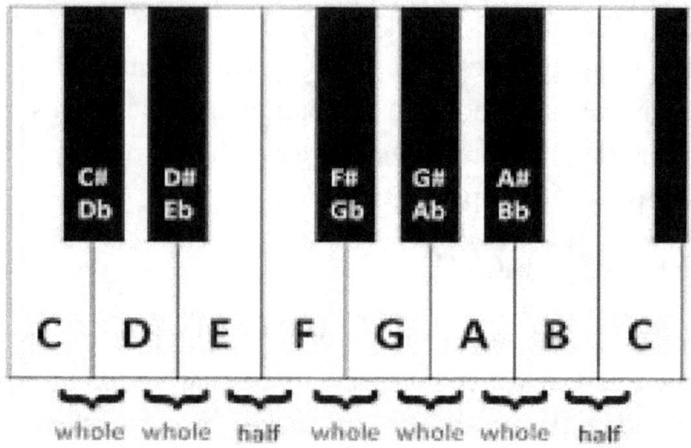

Figure 5.1

For example, we know that the distance from A to A♯ is a half step. The distance between B and B♭ is a half step. In other words, two consecutive half steps form a whole step. The format of any major scale usually follows this kind of sequence:

whole whole half whole whole whole half

This can also be written as:

w w h w w w h

This sequence means that there is a whole step between the first and second note, the second and third note, the fourth and fifth note, the fifth and sixth note, and the sixth and seventh note. There is a half step between the third and fourth note and the seventh and eighth note.

Please memorize this pattern because every major scale you encounter from here onwards will use this same sequence.

So, if we want to form the C major scale, we can write it as:

C w D w E h F w G w A w B h C

Figure 5.2

However, if we want to form the D major scale, we can write it as:

D w E w F♯ h G w A w B w C♯ h D

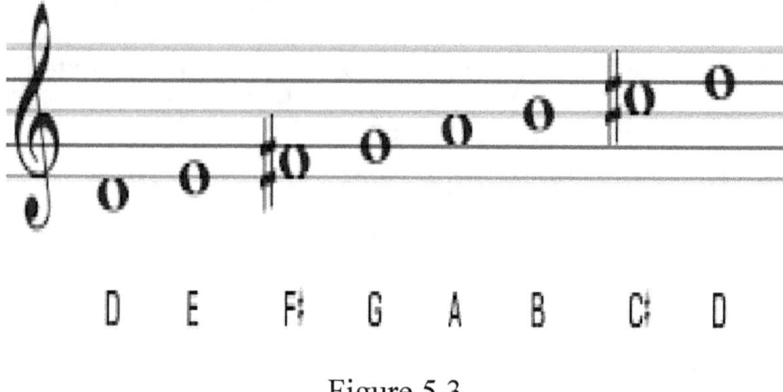

Figure 5.3

Minor Scales

Most people think of minor scales as confusing. This is because many music students usually start learning about the major scale first and end up focusing on it more than the minor scale. This situation isn't helped by the fact that there are a number of different types of minor scales that are often confused with one another. However, we will only focus on the most common minor scale in this book.

It is important to note that a piece of music in a particular major scale will sound the same as music in another major scale. For example, music that is in C major will sound somewhat similar to music in D major.

However, music in D major will sound very different from that in D minor because the notes in a minor scale are arranged in a very different pattern. Music written using a minor key has a sad, ominous, or mysterious sound than that written using a major key.

Natural Minor Scale

A natural minor scale is a scale where every note is played in a minor key signature. A natural minor scale is formed by starting at the tonal centre and moving upward using the following step pattern:

Whole half whole whole half whole whole

w h w w h w w

For example, music written in D minor scale will look like this:

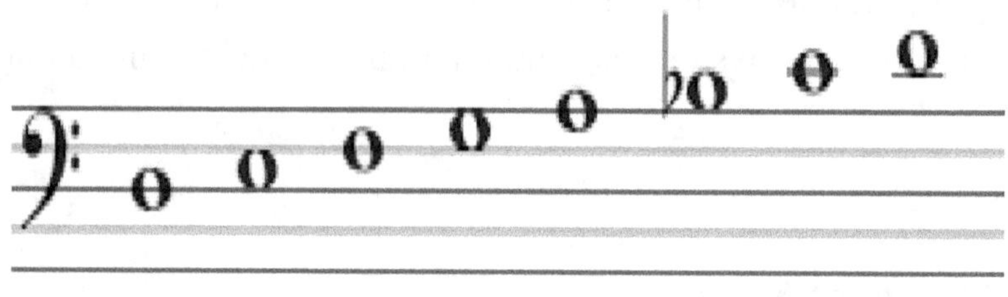

Figure 5.4

Exercise 4

1. Draw a staff with a treble clef. Write down the notes of the A major scale.

2. Draw a staff with a bass clef. Write down the notes of the G flat major scale.

3. Draw a staff with a treble clef. Write down the notes of the F minor scale.

4. Draw a staff with a treble clef. Write down the notes of the A flat minor scale.

Chapter Summary

Here are the key points to remember from this chapter:

- A music scale is a set of notes that sound good together, arranged in sequential order, within a particular piece of music.
- The tonal centre is the first note in a scale and is used to name that particular scale.
- To remember the sequence of notes in a major scale, follow the pattern *w w h w w w h.*
- A natural minor scale is written in a minor key and follows the pattern *w h w w h w w.*

In the next chapter, you will learn about the different types of intervals and how they are built.

Chapter Six: Building Intervals

In this chapter, you will learn about the different types of intervals and how to name them. Intervals are a very important concept in music. In fact, you cannot learn about scales or chords without making some reference to intervals. As a serious student of music theory, you must take the time to learn intervals and how to identify them.

Defining Intervals

An interval can be defined as the distance or space between two notes or pitches. Intervals are described using whole steps and half steps, which we have already covered in the previous chapters. The uncomplicated way to describe an interval would be to say, "E natural is one-half step below F natural," or "A flat is one step and a half away from F."

However, these are small distances. What about when we need to describe longer intervals in a major or minor scale?

How to Name Intervals

The primary factor you have to consider when naming an interval is the distance between the two notes. You need to look at how the notes are presented and then count the spaces and lines between the notes in the staff. Make sure that you include the spaces or lines that the notes are positioned on.

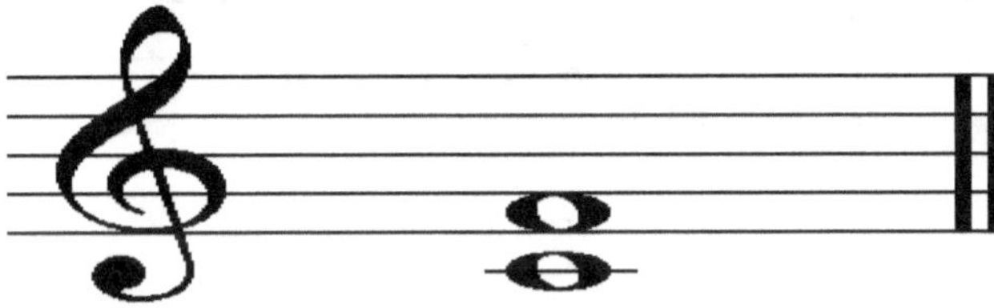

Figure 6.1

Figure 6.2

In figure 6.1 above, the interval between the C and F notes is four. We refer to this *a fourth*. In figure 6.2, the interval count between C and E is a third. At this point, the type of clef, key signature, and accidental (flats and sharps) don't matter.

If the interval between the notes is less or equal to one octave, it is referred to as a **simple interval** *(fig 6.3)*. If the interval is greater than one octave, it is called a **compound interval** *(fig 6.4)*.

Figure 6.3

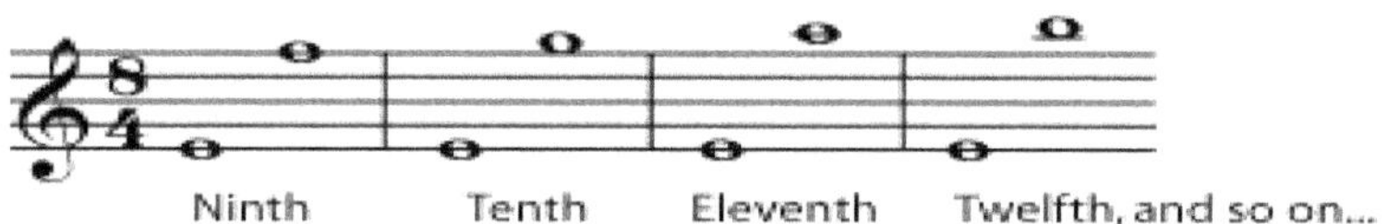

Figure 6.4

Now in the next phase of identifying an interval, we will consider the clef, key signature, and accidentals.

Perfect Intervals

Certain intervals are considered to be perfect intervals. They include primes, fourths, fifths, and octaves. They are called perfect because their sound waves are related very closely to one another. This makes these intervals sound good together.

Another name for a perfect prime is **unison,** which represents two notes that produce the same pitch. A perfect fourth has 5 half steps and a perfect fifth has 7 half steps. A perfect octave is where two notes are eight intervals apart, that is, 12 half steps apart. It is important that you understand how these steps are counted. You can go back and refresh your knowledge from the previous chapter on scales.

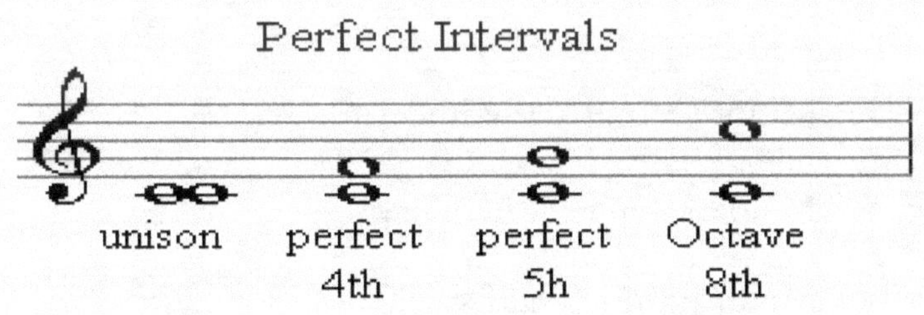

Figure 6.5

Major and Minor Intervals

The rest of the simple intervals form the major and minor intervals. These include seconds, thirds, sixths, and sevenths. A minor interval is one half-step smaller than a major one. They are described as follows:

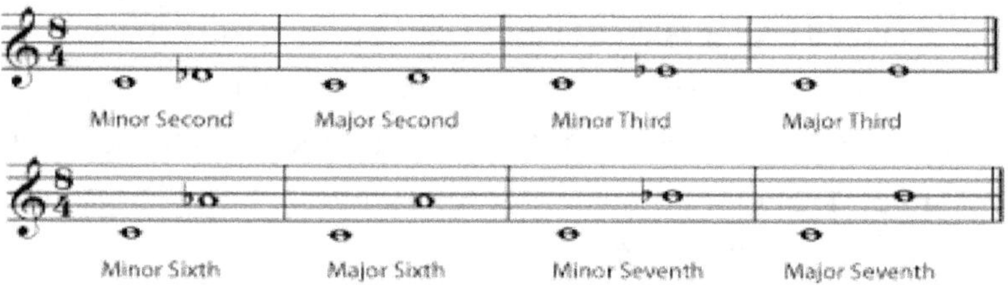

Figure 6.6

- Minor second – 1 half step

- Major second – 2 half steps

- Minor third – 3 half steps

- Major third – 4 half steps

- Minor sixth – 8 half steps

- Major sixth – 9 half steps

- Minor seventh – 10 half steps

- Major seventh – 11 half steps

Exercise 5

1. Give the complete name of the intervals.

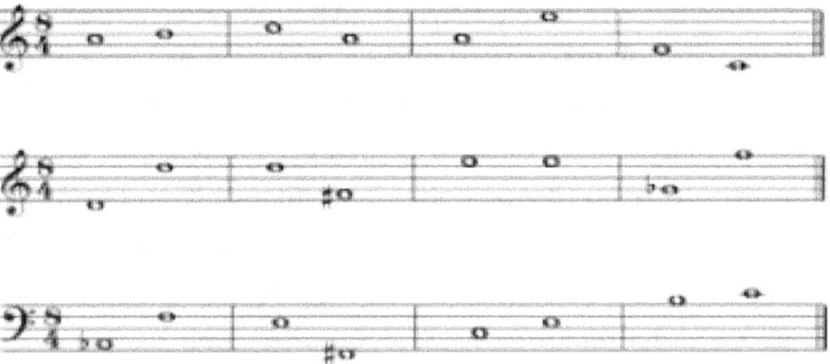

Chapter Summary

Here are the key points that you need to remember:

- Interval is the distance between two pitches.
- In order to name an interval, count the lines and spaces between the two notes. Don't forget to include the line or space the notes are standing on.
- The second phase of naming an interval must consider the half steps. The clef, key signature, and accidentals are important here.
- A simple interval is one octave or smaller, while a compound interval is greater than one octave.
- Intervals are considered perfect if their sound waves are closely related. Perfect intervals include primes, fourths, fifths, and octaves
- A perfect prime is also called unison.
- A minor interval is one half-step smaller than a major interval. These intervals include seconds, thirds, sixths, and sevenths.

In the next chapter, you will learn about key signatures and the circle of fifths.

Chapter Seven: Key Signatures

In this chapter, you will learn about how to use key signatures to make the performance of music much easier. You will also learn about the major and minor key signatures as well as how to read the circle of fifths.

Key signatures are a very important part of music. The key signature is what we use to know the pitches that a song will be performed. Every time that a piece of music is performed, it is played in a particular key or tonality. For example, if a song is to be played using the D key, then the entire song must be based around a D chord or a D note. Even the notes used will be from a D scale. The key signature represents all this information.

So how do we know the key that is being used?

If you look at the beginning of every line of written music, you will notice that there are sharps or flats (also known as accidentals) right after the clef symbol. These accidentals tell us the key to use. It is important to note that a key can either be a sharp or a flat, but it can never be both.

So, what is the significance of using keys? When you are writing a long piece of music in a single key, you will soon find it very tedious to keep repeating the accidentals all over the staff. Look at the image below to see what a simple melody in D major looks like if you don't use a key signature.

Figure 7.1

Now, this is just a short section of a piece of music. If you were writing a full song, the staff would get quite messy, not to mention the fact that you would get tired of writing all those sharps. So, to avoid this, music composers use key signatures only at the beginning of the staff to show the performers which pitches must have accidentals.

Below is the same simple melody in D major. But this time it has a key signature that indicates that the notes C and F should be sharpened.

Figure 7.2

The Circle of Fifths

This is a graphical way of arranging keys to show how closely related they are to each other. The circle of fifths has been part of music theory for centuries, and it provides a great method for summarizing the key signatures to be used for any key that has a maximum of seven sharps or flats.

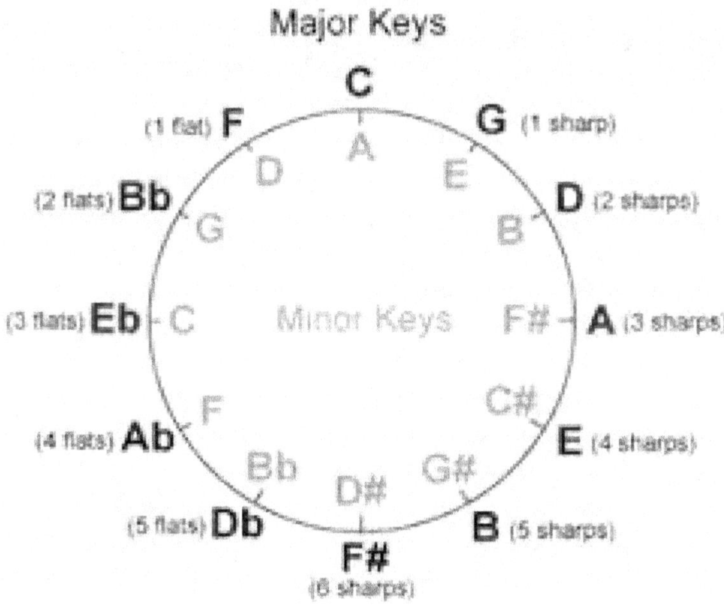

Figure 7.3

So how will you know which notes in the key are supposed to be sharpened or flattened? In order to use the circle of fifths to identify your key signature, you must use a mnemonic device to help you memorize the order of sharps and flats.

The first thing to do is memorize the order of notes on the following circle:

F C G D A E B

Most people use the mnemonic *Father Charles Goes Down And Ends Battle*

If you want to determine the sharp keys, you move clockwise around the circle of fifths. Then you read the mnemonic forward. For example, according to the circle of fifths, there are three sharps in the key A major. But which notes exactly are supposed to be sharp?

Moving clockwise along the circle and following the order of notes, you will identify the notes to be sharpened as F, C, and G.

If you want to determine the flat keys, you must move anticlockwise along the circle, and then read the mnemonic backward. For example, according to the circle of fifths, there are four flats in the key for A-flat major. But which notes should be flattened?

Moving anticlockwise along the circle and backward along the order of notes, you will see that B, E, A, and D are the notes that will have flats.

The reason why we call it a circle of fifths is because as you move from one section (or key) to the next, you are moving down or up by an interval of a perfect fifth. If you move clockwise by a perfect fifth, you will land on a key with one sharp more or one flat less than where you started. If you move anticlockwise a perfect fifth, you land on a key that has one flat more or one sharp less than where you started.

Minor Key Signatures

So far, we have been focusing more on the major keys. However, minor keys also have signatures. Every major key you see on the circle of fifths has a corresponding minor key with the exact same signature. Minor and major keys that have corresponding key signatures are referred to as *relative keys*. For example, both F major and D minor have one flat. F major is regarded as the relative major of D minor while D minor is regarded as the relative minor of F major.

In other words, just because keys are next to each other on a keyboard (the chromatic scale) does not mean that they are closely related. The main factor that determines the relationship is having similar key signatures. The closer the keys are in the circle of fifths, the closer their relationship in terms of key signature.

This means that the next most closely related keys to F major and D minor are C major (or A minor), and B major (or G minor). Those keys that don't correspond at all with the key signature of F major are on the opposite side of the circle.

Exercise 6

1. Which keys in the circle of fifths are closely related to F sharp major and B flat major?

2. Name the major and minor keys for each key signature.

Chapter Summary

Here are the key points to remember:

- Key signatures tell us the pitches that a song will be performed in.
- To make writing music much easier, the key signature is placed at the beginning of the staff instead of between the notes in the staff.
- The accidentals indicate the key to be used in a piece of music.
- The circle of fifths is a graphical illustration of keys and indicates how closely related they are to each other.
- To determine the key being used, look at the number of sharps or flats in the key signature.
- To identify key signatures, use the mnemonic Father Charles Goes Down And Ends Battle (FCGDAEB).
- To identify the sharp keys, move clockwise around the circle and read the mnemonic forwards.
- To identify the flat keys, move anticlockwise and read the mnemonic backward.
- Major and minor keys that have corresponding key signatures are known as relative keys.

In the next chapter, you will learn about triads, chords, and chord progressions.

Chapter Eight: Building Chords

In this chapter, you will learn chords, which are the building blocks of the tone of a piece of music. Learning how to build chords can be a bit challenging for beginners, but the trick lies in taking it one step at a time. For that reason, we are going to focus on building triads, major chords, and minor chords.

Chords

A chord is simply a group of notes that are played together. Most of the sad songs you hear use what are known as minor chords. The upbeat songs tend to use suspended second chords or major seventh chords. Chords can either be used to make melodies or they can be arranged in specific sequences known as progressions to create a sense of direction and movement in music.

Triads

Chords are a set of three or more pitches that are played together. A chord that is made up of three notes that can be arranged as thirds is known as a *triad*. The fastest way to know if a chord of three notes is a triad is to arrange the notes in a circle of thirds. If the pitch classes of the three notes sit next to each other, then they form a triad.

There are two ways of identifying a triad, i.e., according to its root and its quality. The *root of chord,* which is the note that gives the chord its name, is the lowest note. The second note in the triad is known as the *third of chord*, while the last note in the triad is called the *fifth of chord*. After you position the root of chord, you then place the third of chord a third higher than the root. The fifth of chord is then placed a fifth higher than the root, which coincides with a third higher than the third of chord. If you find this confusing, you may need to go to Chapter 6 (figure 6.3) where we learned about intervals.

In the figure below, the chord is written in the root position as a stack of third, which is the easiest way to write down a triad. Don't forget that in most cases, the root is the bottom note, unless you are dealing with an inversion.

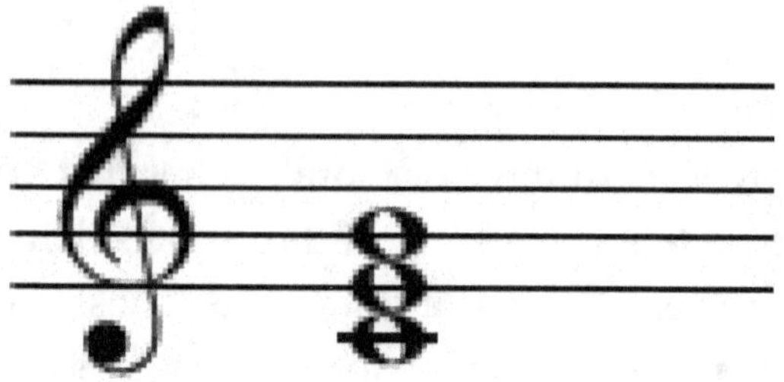

Figure 8.1

First and Second Inversions

First inversion occurs when the third of chord becomes the lowest note. In case the fifth of chord is placed at the bottom, then the chord is said to be in *second inversion*. The second inversion is also known as a *six-four chord* because the intervals are a sixth and a fourth.

The most important factor in a chord is not the distance between the top two notes from the lowest note. The number of notes also isn't an issue. The thing that matters the most is which note is at the bottom.

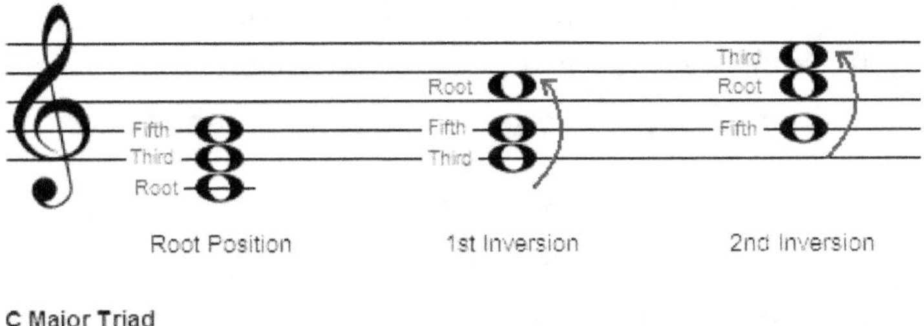

Figure 8.2

Triad Qualities

The first step in determining the quality of a triad is to identify the interval between the root and the other notes in the chord. The four qualities of triads that can be found in major and minor scales include:

- Major triad – M3 and P5 above root

- Minor triad – m3 and p5 above root

- Diminished triad – m3 and d5 above root

- Augmented triad – M3 and A5 above root

The two most common triads are the major and minor chords. In these two types of chords, the root of the chord and fifth of chord are at an interval of a perfect fifth, which are 7 half steps. This interval can be split into a major third, which is 4 half-steps, and a minor third, which forms 3 half-steps.

A ***major chord*** is formed when the major third falls between the root and the third of chord. A ***minor chord*** is formed when the minor third falls between the root and the third of chord.

On the other hand, diminished and augmented chords do not have a perfect fifth, which explains why they produce an anxious feeling in listeners. **Augmented chords** are formed when two major thirds are combined, thus creating an augmented fifth. **Diminished chords** are formed when two minor thirds are combined, thus creating a diminished fifth.

Figure 8.3

Seventh Chords

This is a chord that is formed when you take a triad and combine it with a note that is a seventh above the root. There are many different varieties of seventh chords, and we distinguish them according to the type of seventh and type of triad used. Here are some of the most common types of seventh chords:

- Dominant seventh chord – This is a combination of a major triad and a minor seventh

- Minor seventh chord – This is a combination of a minor triad and a minor seventh

- Major seventh chord – This is a combination of a major triad and a major seventh

- Diminished seventh chord – This is a combination of a diminished triad and a diminished seventh

- Half-diminished seventh chord – This is a combination of a diminished triad and a minor seventh

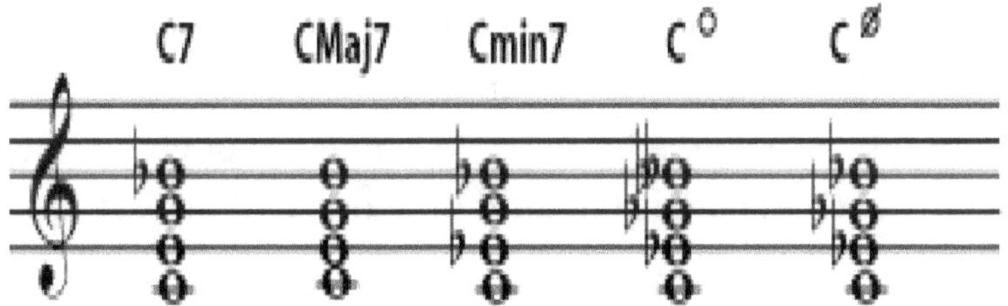

Figure 8.4

Exercise 7

1. Write these seventh chords – G minor seventh; B flat major seventh; F sharp minor seventh; and D diminished seventh.

Chapter Summary

Here are some of the key points that you need to remember:

- A chord is a group of notes that are played together.
- A chord that comprises three notes arranged as thirds is known as a triad.
- Its root and quality can identify a triad.
- In a triad, the lowest note is the root of chord; the second note is the third of chord, and the last note is the fifth of chord.
- First inversion occurs when the third of chord becomes the lowest note.
- Second inversion occurs when the fifth of chord becomes the lowest note.
- When the interval between the root and third of chord is the major third, a major chord is formed.
- When the interval between the root and third of chord is the minor third, a major chord is formed.

- When two major thirds are combined, an augmented chord is formed.
- When two minor thirds are combined, a diminished chord is formed.
- A seventh chord is formed when you add a triad and a note that is a seventh above the root.

Final Words

You have come to the end of the book. Though it was a long journey, I'm sure you now have a much better understanding of music theory than before. If you had never studied the subject previously, you should be ready to move on to the more complex theories of music. If you already had a background in music, then your knowledge of music theory will help you become an even better musician. For those who were seeking a refresher course in some of the elements you had forgotten, consider your mind refreshed.

Music theory is not really as hard as it looks or sounds. The bottom line is that you have to have a solid foundation that will always be there to guide you. The seven elements of music we have covered in this book are the keys to unlocking any musical composition. On top of that, there are seven good exercises in this book that will help you crystallize the knowledge you have gained in each chapter.

The questions provided in every exercise have covered the fundamentals that every music student and musician must know like the back of their hand. If you were keen when reading the book, I'm sure you had an easy time answering them. If you felt like you were struggling a little bit, then don't worry about it. Just go back to the chapter where you feel uncertain and reread it. Some of the concepts usually take time to sink in. Don't forget that the answers to every question are on the last page of the book.

Being able to read and write music is a very rewarding experience, and now you are ready to move onto the next phase of your musical journey. Yes, that was the easy part. Anybody can buy a book, read it, and toss it aside. All it will cost you is some time and money. However, you must now do the hard work necessary to integrate and incorporate this new knowledge into your music. This book has provided you with an opportunity to learn something that can help you going forward. Don't stop here. What is important is that you continue to practice and challenge yourself. Never stop learning and always make an effort to put into practice everything that you have learned in this book.

I am honoured that you took the time to read this book. It was a pleasure for me to walk with you through your musical journey. I hope you enjoyed reading and learning from this beginner's guide to music theory.

Thank you and good luck!

Solutions to Exercise Questions

Solutions to Exercise 1

1. Draw the staff on a piece of paper and practice writing the two clef symbols on the staff. Draw as many as you can until you learn it perfectly.

2. Draw the staff with a treble clef and name all the spaces on the staff.

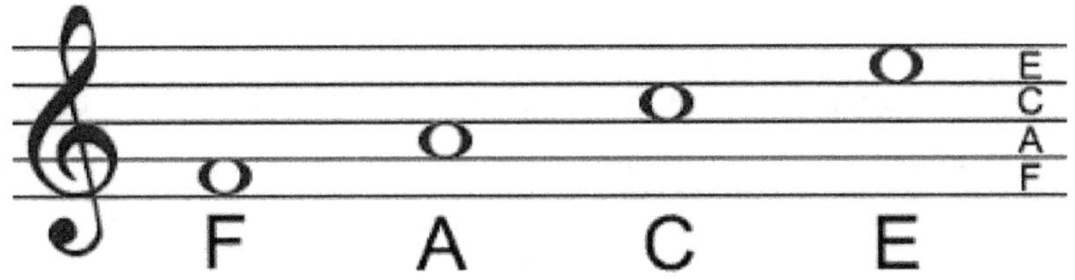

3. Draw the staff with a bass clef and name all the lines on it.

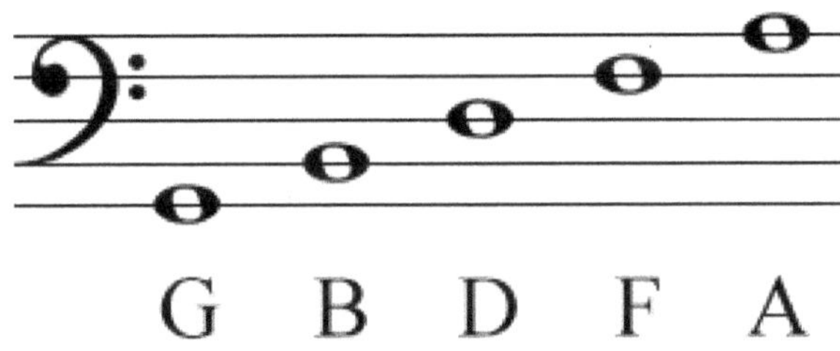

4. On a staff with a treble clef, name the ledger lines and spaces above the staff.

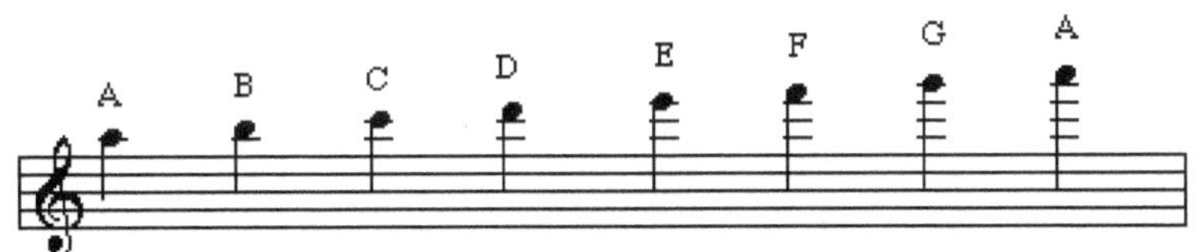

5. On a staff with a bass clef, name the ledger lines and
   spaces below the staff.

Solutions to Exercise 2

1. Complete the following series of natural notes: A B C D
    E F G A

2. Provide an alternative name for the following:

A♯ - B ♭

D♭ - C♯

G♭ - F♯

E♭ - D♯

3. 1 semibreve = 8 quavers

4. 1 minim = 4 quarters

5. 1 minim = 1 quarter + 2 eighths

6. Three staves with a treble clef symbol and time
    signatures showing *two four time*, *three eight time,* and
    six four time. Fill in each measure with a different
    combination of note lengths. Use at least one dotted note
    per staff.

Solutions to Exercise 3

1. Italian tempo markings:

    - Poco piu mosso – a little more movement/motion

    - Piu vivo – more lively

    - Un poco allegro – a little fast

    - Molto adagio – very slow

2. In order from quietest to loudest: pp, mp, p, f, mf, ff

Solutions to Exercise 4

1. The staff with a treble clef and notes of the A major scale.

2. The staff with a bass clef and notes of the G flat major scale.

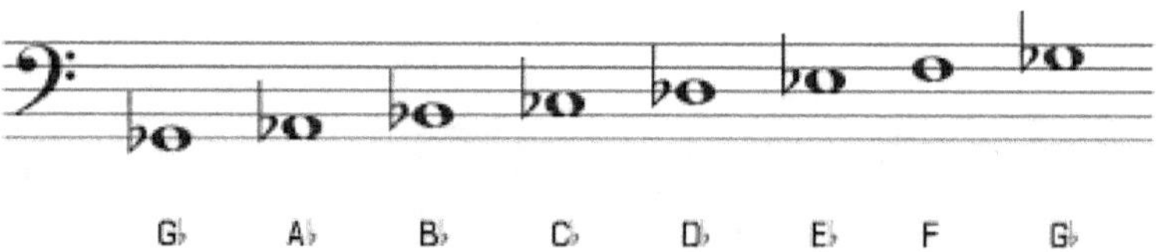

3. The staff with a treble clef and notes of the F minor scale.

F minor scale

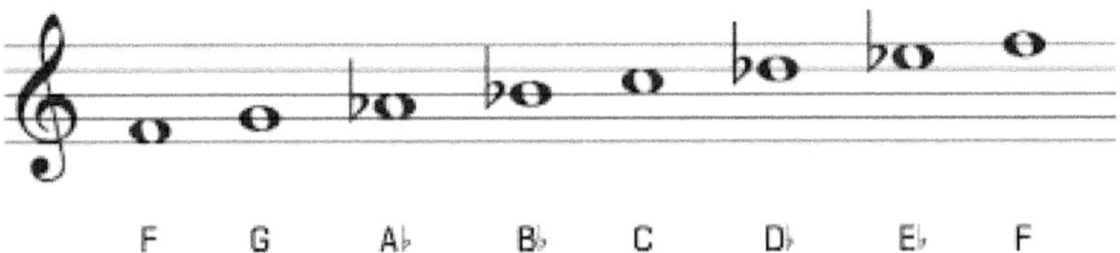

4. The staff with a treble clef and notes of the A flat minor scale.

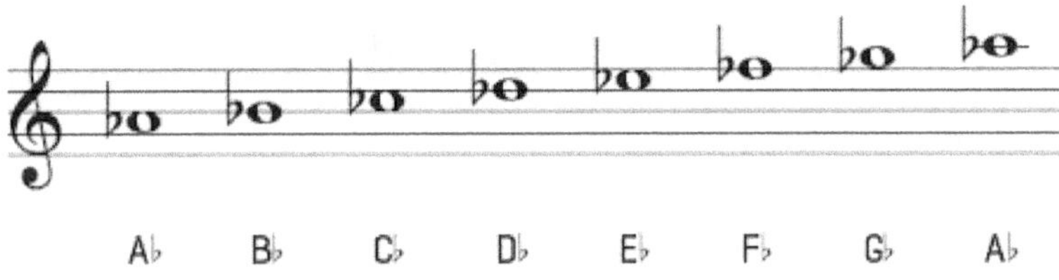

Solutions to Exercise 5

Names of intervals:

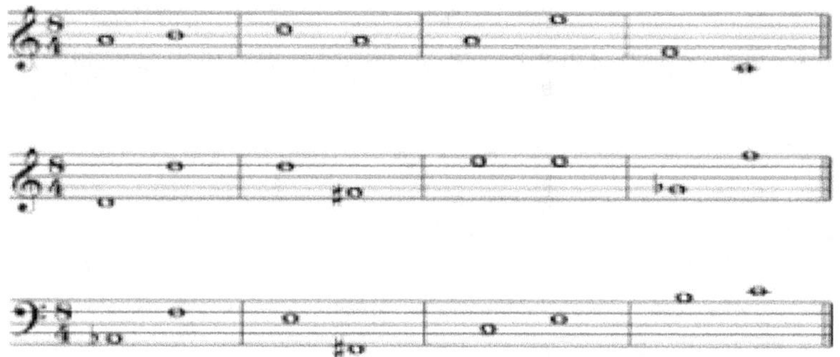

Top Staff:

Major Second - Minor Third - Perfect Fifth - Perfect Fourth

Centre Staff:

Perfect Octave – Minor Sixth – Perfect Prime (Unison) – Major Seventh

Bottom Staff:

Major Sixth – Minor Seventh – Major Third – Minor Second

Solution to Exercise 6

1.   Relative keys to:

 F sharp major – D sharp minor

B flat major – G minor

2.   Major and minor keys for each key signature:

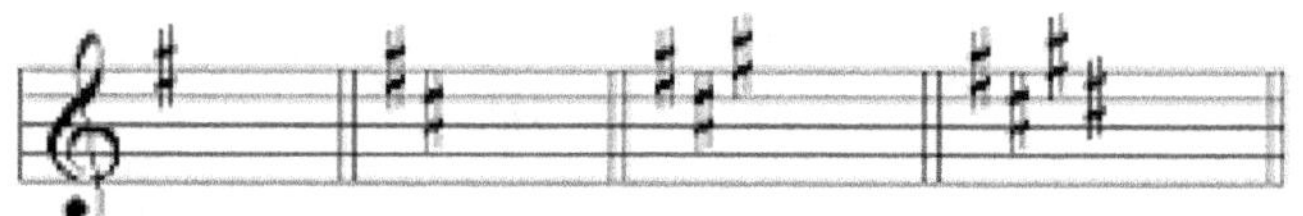

G Major – D Major – A Major – E Major

Solutions to Exercise 7

G minor 7th chord

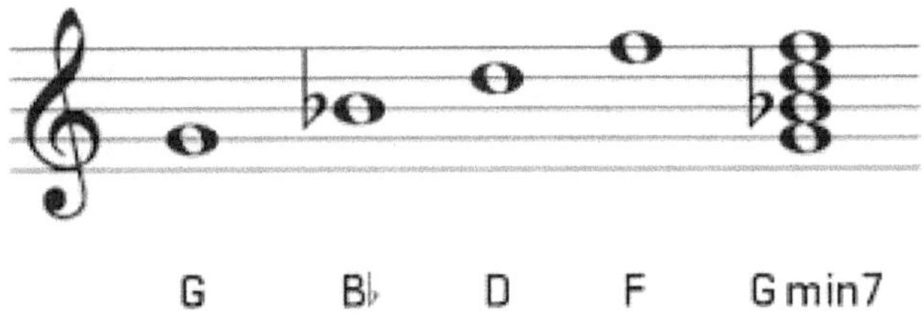

B-flat major 7th chord

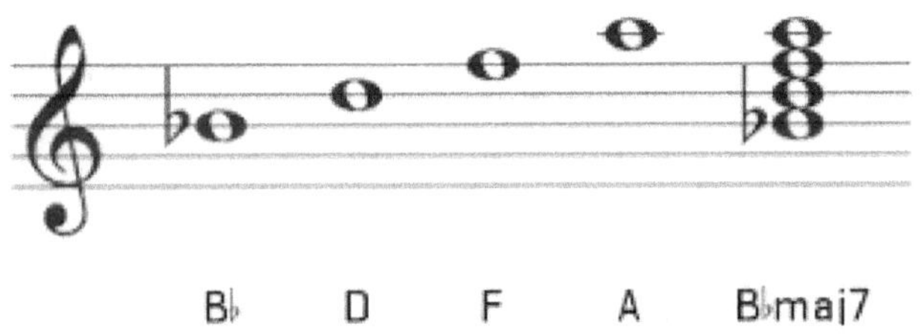

F-sharp minor 7th chord

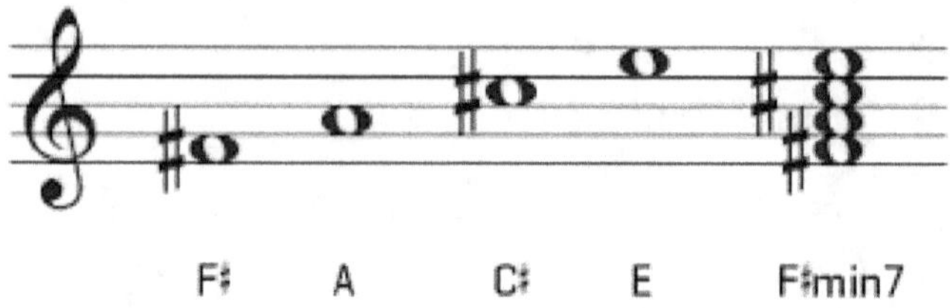

D diminished 7th chord

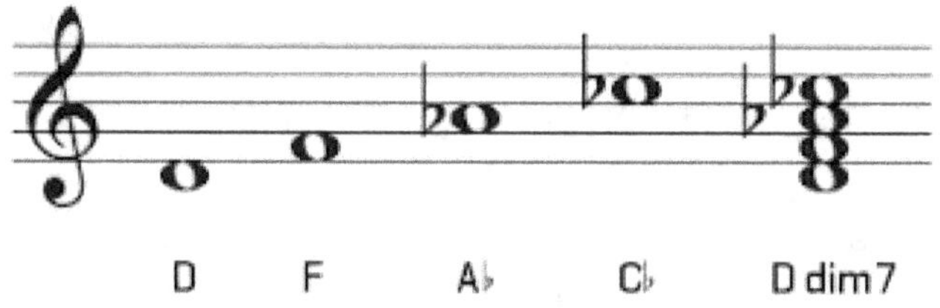

HOW TO PLAY
CHORDS
IN 1 DAY
The Only 7 Exercises You
Need to Learn Guitar Chords, Piano
Chords and Ukulele Chords Today
PRESTON HOFFMAN

BOOK 2

HOW TO PLAY CHORDS: IN 1 DAY

The Only 7 Exercises You Need to Learn Guitar Chords, Piano Chords and Ukulele Chords Today

Preston Hoffman

Table of Contents

Chapter One: Know Your Instruments

Welcome to your handy-dandy guide to learning how to play chords on the guitar, ukulele, and piano! It may come as a surprise—or it may not—to learn that all three of these instruments are quite easy to learn and you can quickly play thousands of songs on them just by following a few simple exercises and learning about the basic chords. But first, we need to break down the differences between these three instruments, since playing them will be slightly different for the chords and for your hands.

The Guitar

The guitar is the world's most popular instrument, and for good reason. It's versatile, easily portable, works well with other instruments, and is easy to learn—as you're about to find out. It has a wide range and is great for people who also enjoy singing, since you can easily play the guitar while you sing and it accompanies voices well.

There are many different types of guitars, the two main categories being acoustic and electric. It's recommended that you start with an acoustic guitar.

This here is an acoustic guitar:

And this is an electric guitar:

But there are variations within that, as well, like nylon versus steel strings, for example. Nylon strings are more mellow and easier on your fingers, while steel strings produce a bright tone and are louder. They're also harder on your fingers.

These here are nylon strings:

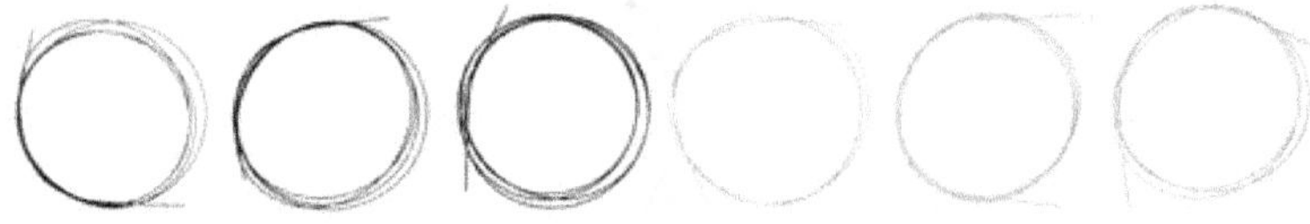

And these here are steel strings:

If those two images don't look too different to you, it's because the nylon is wrapped in either bronze-plated copper or in silver wire. If you're just looking at strings on a guitar, you might not be able to tell the difference at first. But you'll feel the difference in your fingers when you play them.

The best type of guitar for a beginner is a steel-strung guitar with round holes in the sideboards. They're the best for playing most of the songs you'll come across, including all of the songs in this book, and they create a good sound for accompanying singers and other instruments.

Another type of guitar is the Jumbo Guitar. It has an extra-large body, which means that it produces a better bass sound. If you're a bass player in a band, this might be the type of guitar you'd go for. This is a great guitar but with twelve strings and a larger body, it's not good for beginners:

It can be hard to see in this image, but where on a regular acoustic guitar like the one above each of the notches only has one string, these have two. Definitely not easy on your hands and the added musical value won't be of use to you until much later when you're further down the line in your understanding of music and can start to play around with the melodies of your songs instead of just focusing on the chords, which is what we're doing in this book.

Flamenco and Classical Guitars are strung with nylon and are used specifically for flamenco and classical music, respectively. They're good guitars and easy to learn on as a beginner but since they're for specialized music, you won't want to use them unless you're planning on playing mainly classical music.

There might not seem to be much of a difference in these guitars when you look at them, but it's all in the tuning. Flamenco guitars are designed to have a higher note register and the strings are therefore slightly different to accommodate this. Regular acoustic guitars have a lower register.

A classical guitar, on the other hand, will have a wider fret board, which can make it difficult for newer players to reach all of the strings, and they don't always have fret markers to help you out. Classical guitars just aren't designed for modern-day pop songs. Trying to play a Beatles song, for example, or that guitar classic "Wonderwall" on a classic guitar would just make it sound weird. So for our purposes, unless you want to play more classical music or more folk-sounding music, stick to regular acoustic.

Note: "Wonderwall" is considered one of the most overplayed songs on guitar, so it's best to avoid playing it.

Finally, electric guitars are the kind of guitars that can only be played when you plug them into an amplifier. You can attach pedals and other instruments to help play around with the sound of them. They're great for jazz and rock, but they might not be a good bet for a beginner. If you know your way around a guitar and want to start picking up some fancy tricks, new ways to play with sound, or you're joining a band and want to be able to be heard, then you can get an electric guitar.

Be sure to take good care of your guitar! Buy a sturdy case for it and store it in there. Hang onto the receipt after you buy it in case you're traveling with it and need to show the receipt to customs. Never let your guitar lie in the grass or dirt and be careful with it around moisture.

The Ukulele

There are, as you can tell just by looking at them, a lot of similarities between a ukulele and a guitar. However, there are also some differences to keep in mind.

First, there are the four types of ukulele: soprano, alto, tenor, and baritone—yes, just like singing voices. The soprano is the smallest, and the easiest to start out with as a beginner, since it has only four strings. The baritone is the largest and most expensive, and personally, if you're looking at a baritone then at that point you might just want to get a guitar instead.

Here is a soprano ukulele:

Here is an alto ukulele:

This is a tenor ukulele:

And finally, a baritone ukulele:

The ukulele will always sound a bit higher than the guitar, so it's natural when you're learning a song on the ukulele versus guitar for it to sound a bit higher—but the notes should still sound *right*. You'll find that it's easy for your ear to pick up the difference between notes played correctly at a higher pitch and notes that are played incorrectly. Fortunately, it's actually simpler to play chords on a ukulele than a guitar, so now that we've got you on the guitar, you'll find the transition to ukulele is pretty easy.

The most notable difference in a ukulele versus a guitar will be the strings. The tuning for a ukulele is usually GCEA:

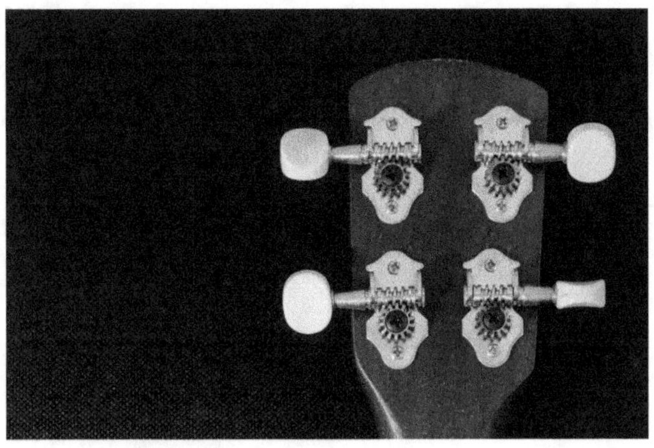

To compare this to a guitar, put a capo on the 5th fret of a guitar. A "capo" is a bar that you can buy that will hold down all of the strings on a particular fret for you. This will come in handy when you've progressed further and are performing songs where you're doing chords but can't have a finger free to hold down all the strings. With the capo on the 5th fret, play the four highest strings on your guitar. That's what it's like to play a ukulele, except that the G string on the ukulele is an octave higher even than that.

Baritone ukuleles, however, are exactly the same as the four highest strings on the guitar, no capo needed. This is why it's probably best not to buy a baritone ukulele—any song that you'd play on there you can just play on the guitar by ignoring the two lowest strings.

The Piano

The piano is probably the best known, and most beloved, of all musical instruments. Many composers started composing their pieces on piano to start with, before adding in the other instruments, and it's a versatile instrument that can handle pretty much any song that you throw at it.

A piano is, technically, a string instrument. When you press down on a key, you're actually starting up a mechanism that causes the string or strings to be plucked, causing the sound. It's also one of the most complicated instruments in the world, with 2,500 parts, and it's easily broken. The many parts of a piano include the soundboard, ribs, bridges, keys, pedals, hammers, the strings, and the cast iron plate.

Yes, a cast iron plate. It's put in over the soundboard of the piano and anchors the strings and keeps them tense so that they will vibrate properly when plucked by the hammer, which is caused by pressing on a key. The largest kind of piano is the grand piano:

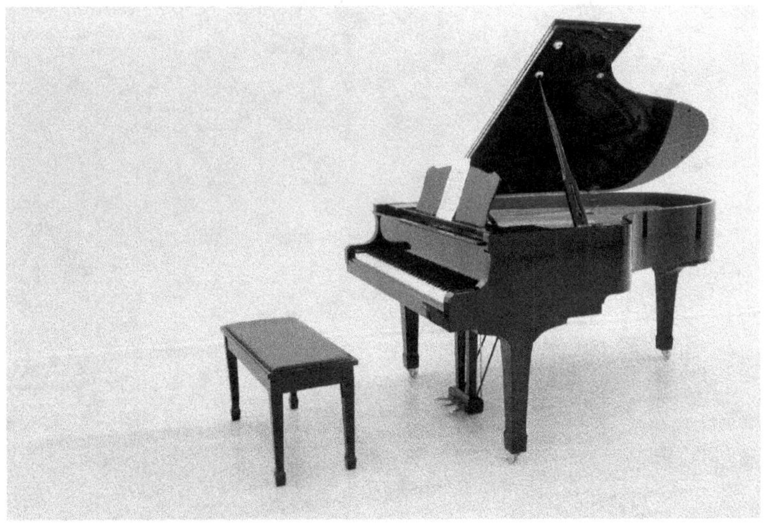

These are also known as winged pianos and are the largest in size. You would need a rather large home to fit one of these. The next smallest is the baby grand piano, structured in every way like a grand piano, only with smaller dimensions:

The other kind of piano, and the one that most people can afford both economically and size-wise, is an upright piano:

And finally, we have the electric keyboard, the least expensive and most convenient for when you're living in a small house:

Unless you're living in an area where you have access to a grand or a baby grand, you don't need to worry about practicing on one. Practicing on a keyboard or upright piano will give you the same kind of understanding and practice, and if you're looking to perform, those are the two kinds of pianos that you'll most likely be performing on when the time comes.

Now that you understand your instruments, it's time to learn how to play them!

Chapter Two: What are Chords?

Chords are the basis for an entire song or piece of music. Without chords, you don't have a song, which is why if you know the chords of a song, you can play those same four or so notes over and over again in the rhythm of the song without learning the rest, and the audience will still recognize said song. By learning the chords through the exercises this book will teach, you'll be able to play thousands of songs. But what exactly are chords and how do they work?

What Is a Chord?

A chord is a combination of three or more notes. They're built off of a single note, known as the 'root note.' The root note will always be the first note in the chord sequence. So if you see the chord sequence C-E-G, that's a C chord. Those three notes together create a harmonious, blended sound, called the chord. When you're playing chords, whether it's guitar or piano or ukulele, you create the song by keeping your fingers in the same position, just moving them slightly up or down—so you're always playing the same notes, just as a higher or lower pitch.

How to Read Guitar and Ukulele Chords

Reading guitar and ukulele music is a bit different than reading piano music. Piano tends to use sheet music—which is important to know as a guitarist, because you'll have to read sheet music a lot of the time. Sheet music is the foundation on which all music is written, even if that music is later translated into another form, like guitar tabs.

Guitar tabs function for guitar and ukulele the way sheet music does for a piano. In fact, you can read the tabs without actually having to learn sheet music. This is part of why it's so easy to learn guitar and ukulele (and you can transfer this knowledge to the piano, as we'll discuss shortly).

Tabs are, essentially, a visual representation of where the notes are on the guitar or ukulele that you should be playing:

```
e——————————————  e—————————————O—
B——————————————  B————————O———
G——————————————  G—————O————
D——————————————  D————O—————
A——————————————  A———O——————
E——————————————  E—O————————
```

The strings on the guitar (if this was a ukulele, there would only be four strings) have the thickest, the E string, at the bottom, and the thinnest, the e string, at the top. If there is a number next to the letter, say, a 5 next to the D, that means you're placing your finger on the 5th fret of the D string. If there's a zero, that means the string is being played 'open' with no frets pressed down.

Look at that graphic again. A helpful way to remember the notes is to make an acronym for them. The one I learned was Every August Dogs Go Biting Elvis. E-A-D-G-B-E.

This is another diagram of how guitar chords might be written. The three black dots on the diagram show you which strings to press down—in this case, strings D, G, and B—and you will press down on them on the second fret. The E and A strings we're going to play open, without any frets pressed down, and the High E, or e, we're not going to play at all.

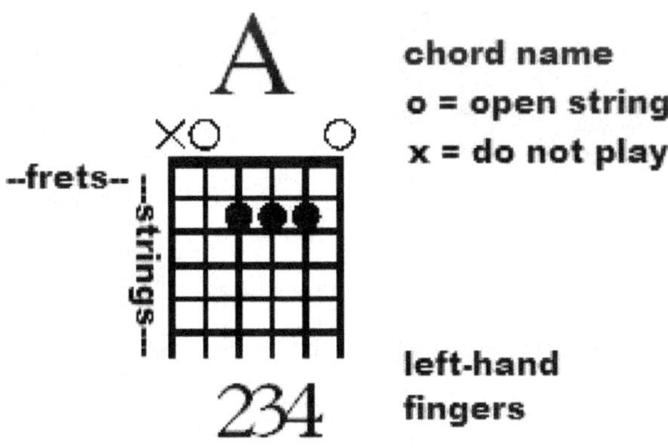

The numbers at the bottom of this chart are telling you which fingers to use to hold down the strings. Your index finger is number one, and your pinkie is number four. So for this, you'll use your middle, ring, and pinkie finger, and leave your index finger free. Keep in mind that your thumb doesn't come into play with the guitar. You use your thumb to brace against the back of the guitar so that it holds still while you move your other fingers. Here's an example of proper finger positioning:

Notice how the thumb is out of sight, bracing on the back of the guitar. The wrist is pushed forward which makes for an angle that will take some getting used to. The fingers, as you can see, are in position, so your index finger (number one) is stretching up to hit the top string.

Let's go back to that chart. So you'd put your middle finger, the 2 finger, on the D string, your ring finger, or 3 finger, on the G string, and your pinkie or 4 finger on the B string, all on the second fret. Use the tips of your fingers only! Otherwise you'll press down on other strings and the sound will come out muffled. Then strum with your other hand. Ta-da! You're now able to read a ukulele or guitar chart and figure out what to play.

The only difference in reading between a ukulele and a guitar is that there are only four strings on a ukulele, so there's just two fewer strings to worry about. But the finger positioning and how you read the chart is all the same.

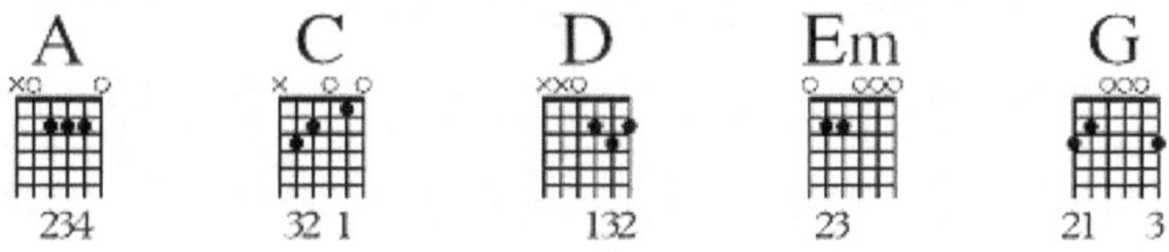

Take a look at these. We have the first one, the A chord, and now the C, D, Em, and G chords. Take a moment and figure out where your fingers go to practice reading it.

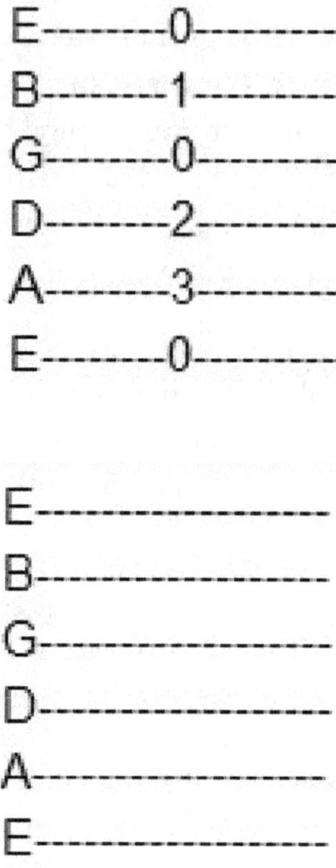

Now, look at the tabs again. The one on the right has no numbering. The one on the left has the numbering showing the fret you want to put your finger on. Unlike the previous chart, it doesn't tell you which finger—so we go with the basic principle of highest string goes to the index finger, second highest to the middle finger, and so on. For this one, you'd have your middle finger on the first fret of the B string, your ring finger on the second fret of the D string, and your pinkie on the third fret of the A string.

It's important to know these tabs because they'll help you for reading sheet music, and moving your chord exercises from guitar to the piano.

Piano Versus Guitar Chords

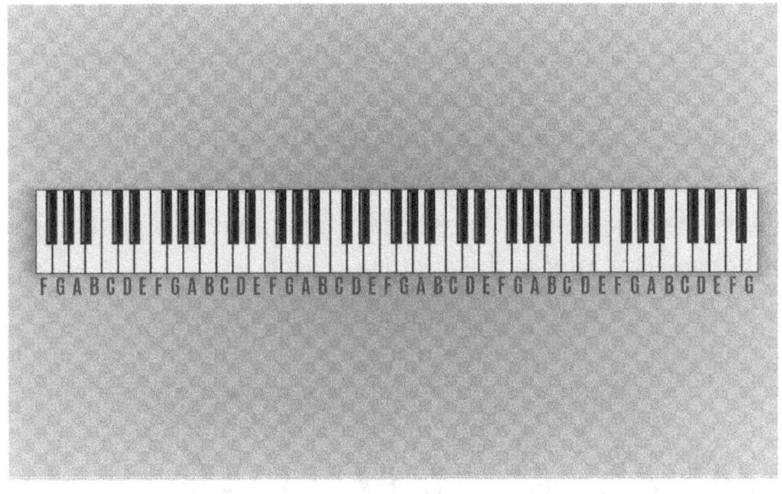

Ah, pianos. You've got a lot more room to work with than guitars, which is both a blessing and a curse when you're a beginner. Take a look at the image up above. Right away you'll notice that it has all of the notes laid out for you. Unlike a guitar, where you create the higher and lower notes by pressing down on the frets, the piano does that for you already. This means that you can play more complicated songs on the piano but it also means your fingers are going to be exhausted.

The key with playing the piano is to stretch your fingers and to keep your wrist light. This is very different from a guitar. In a guitar, if I were to grab your wrist and tug, your wrist shouldn't move. It should be firm to support the guitar neck and your fingers. A piano is the opposite—your wrist should be completely loose and relaxed to allow your fingers the most freedom of movement. If I were to press down on your wrist while you were playing piano, it should collapse.

Keep in mind as well that with both guitar and piano, each finger must move simultaneously. You will be fighting against instinct here. We have trained ourselves to treat our fingers as one unit, to pick things up, to throw things, and so on. Typing is arguably the only thing where our fingers move independently of one another. But look at this picture below:

Note how the thumb is down on the keyboard but the other fingers are not. The thumb is moving independently of the others. If you move one finger on a piano or guitar, the other fingers shouldn't move at all.

Take a look at this picture:

Notice how the hands seem to dip down a little from the wrist, and the fingers are slightly curled. Like with guitar, you want your fingertips to be the ones making the notes, not your whole hand. See how relaxed the wrist is to allow the hand to droop like that? With the guitar, it's all about wrist strength. With piano, it's about wrist relaxation. But with both, remember, you need fingertips and finger flexibility.

Now, like guitar, a piano chord is any set of three or more notes played simultaneously. Note the image below:

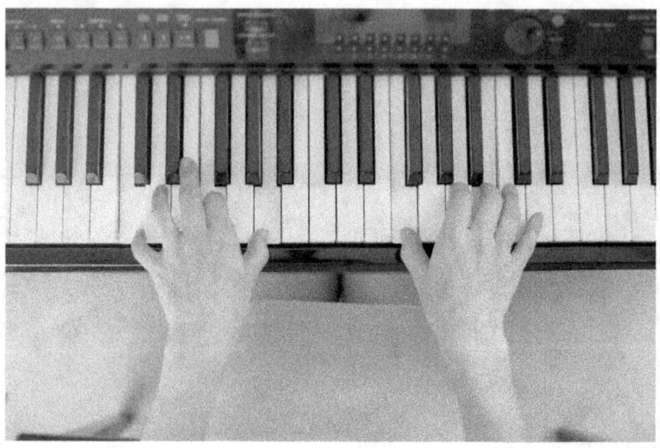

The person's fingers are pressing down on keys while there is are white keys in between them. The thumb, middle finger, and pinkie of the person's right hand are pressing down on the white keys. This creates a chord the same way you do on a guitar. Most piano chords, and certainly these basic ones, will be made with your thumb, middle finger, and pinkie.

The person's left hand is doing the same thing—here is where you can get in some variation. In a guitar, for example, when you're playing the four or five notes with just your one hand, using all of your fingers. As you can see from the image above, those same four or five notes are played with both of your hands. Pressing down on the notes with both hands will create the chord for a piano, while strumming with one hand while the other holds down the strings creates the chord for a guitar or ukulele.

Now, fingers are numbered when you play piano, just like with the guitar. The only difference is that the thumb is included with piano, so instead of the index finger being number one, the thumb is number one, and you go on with the pinkie being number five. So most chords are 1-3-5 chords, using your thumb, middle finger, and pinkie, on three alternating notes.

Alternating is something you're going to come up against in both piano and guitar/ukulele. Now, there are half-steps and full-steps in notes. In a piano, a half-step is when you go from a white key to a black key, or vice versa. You're going from one note to the one directly above or below it. So if you're on the white key C, then go up to the nearest black key, C#, that's a half step. A full-step is where you go up two notes, or one 'full note.' You're not going up from a C to a C sharp or down to a C flat. It's just a full note, so from C to D—which is the next white key.

The only exception? When you're going from white key E. The F key is the same thing as an E#.

All you need to worry about, though, is that when making your chords go from guitar to piano, you put your thumb, or 1 finger, on the root note. Let's say it's C. You would then count up two full-steps. So you'd count up: C#, then D, then D#, then E. So you put your middle finger on E. Then count up two more full-steps: E, F/E#, then F#, to put your pinkie on G.

Now you have the C chord, C-E-G. This is called a major chord, by the way. A minor chord is the opposite. You would put your thumb on C, then go up only one full-step and one half-step, so you wouldn't go all the way up to E—you'd stop at D#. Then you'd put your pinkie on the same place, G. An easy way to remember this? Just put your fingers in position for the chord, then move your middle finger up one half-step.

This is an easy way to have fun with songs, by the way. Play any chord song, but move your middle finger up so that it's now in minor key. It'll sound cool and unusual and completely change how the song sounds.

Another way to help with figuring out the differences in your hands on the piano versus your one hand on the guitar is to imagine the three lowest guitar strings as what you play with your left hand on the piano, and the three highest strings as what you play with your right hand. So let's say you've got your five fingers on five strings on the guitar. Your left hand would take some of those notes, while your right hand would take the others, on the piano. You're just dividing up the notes in a different way, but you still play them all at the same time. A good rule of thumb is that your left hand on the piano plays the root note (so C, for C-E-G), and your right hand plays the others.

But what about sheet music?

That right there probably looks very intimidating. Never fear, though, you won't be learning any of that here—in fact, you won't have to. If you want to play more complicated, classical pieces, then you can learn those once you've mastered these basics, but we're here to learn chords that will allow you to sit down and play the songs that come on the radio. This will, in turn, give you the basic understanding that you'll need if you want to play these more complicated pieces but in the meantime, you'll make a killing serving as the human jukebox for your friends. So, sheet music!

This is a piece of blank sheet music. The first thing you should notice should already be familiar to you—the lines are just like the guitar strings on the guitar tabs we just learned. These lines are called the staff or staves, by the way. This is where you'll see the notes, rather like where you'll see the notations on the tab for which fret to hold down. However, unlike the tabs, which just tell you which fret, notes will tell you how long to hold the note for, so you can look at the sheet music and learn the rhythm even if you don't previously know the song.

This symbol here on the left is called a clef. This indicates the pitch of the notes that you're playing. F, C, and G are the usual types of clef. This here is a G clef, the one you'll probably recognize the most easily.

This here is an F clef.

And this:

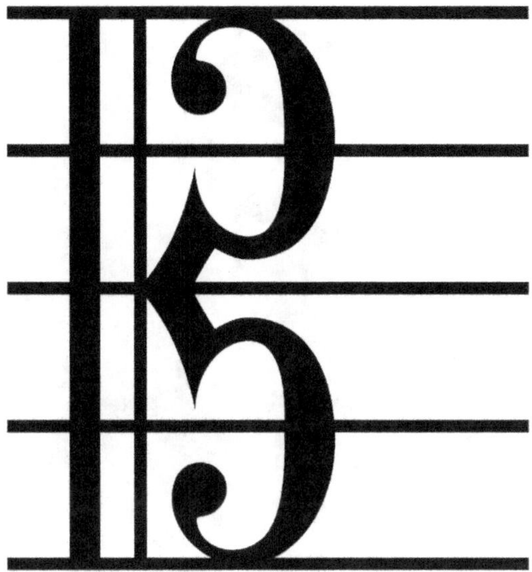

    Is a C clef. The G clef is the one that you'll come across the most often. You probably haven't even seen a C clef before. As you noticed in the image of the blank sheet music, there's a G and an F clef. A G clef is also known as a treble clef, and indicates higher notes, which is why it's higher on the lines. The F clef is also known as a bass clef and means lower notes. You won't often have to deal with such lower notes on your chords, not unless you choose to make your song lower in pitch.

    But what are those symbols next to that image of the G clef? Those are 'key signatures.' They indicate how many sharps and flats are in a piece. You won't often need these but they can be helpful when you're going to play a chord to remember this when you're trying to remember which note is which that you're playing.

This symbol here is a sharp.

And this symbol is a flat.

Note that you'll run into sharps more than you'll run into flats. So if you're playing and you see a letter with one of these symbols after it, it will tell you to place your finger on the white key, and then either move it up a half-step to the nearest black key (a sharp) or down a half-step to the nearest black key (a flat).

The number of sharps and flats next to a clef will tell you what key the piece of music is in. The position of the flats and sharps tells you whether it's an F sharp or a G sharp or so on, and judging by how many there are and what position they're in you'll be able to know what key signature this is in.

This is helpful to keep in the back of your mind for playing classical pieces, but again, it's not necessary for knowing how to play the chords for songs.

Go back and look at the image of the blank sheet music again. You'll see that it ends at the edge of a page. This is called a bar. It will tell you that the measure, or period of time for this part of the music, is over. The number of beats per measure can vary, but there will be however many notes on the sheet music as there are beats, and then at the end there will be the bar. So if you're trying to figure out how many notes are in a measure, count the notations, and when you've reached the bar, you know how many there are—if you counted eight, then there are eight, and so on. The more notes, the faster the piece.

Unlike a guitar or ukulele, where you have to know the song to know how the rhythm goes, the piano music will tell you.

This is a whole note. You hold it four a count of four:

This is a half note. You hold it for a count of two:

This is an ordinary note. Technically it's a quarter note, but it's the most common note that you'll find. You hold it for a single beat:

Sometimes you'll run into these notes:

This dot serves as a half beat. Normally, you're multiplying and dividing by two—a quarter note is one beat, a half note is two beats, and a whole note is four beats. When you see a dot next to this, it means add half of the note's value. So this dot is next to a quarter note, meaning you add half a beat. If it were next to a half note, you'd add one beat, making the entire note three beats long.

This is an eighth note:

As you can imagine, eighth notes are very short, half a beat. They are always half a beat, unlike dots, which can change in value based on the note they're next to. A dot is half the value of the note it's next to, so the value of the dot changes depending on whether it's accompanying a quarter or whole or half note. An eighth note is always half a beat, no matter what other note it's with.

If you ever see a symbol like this:

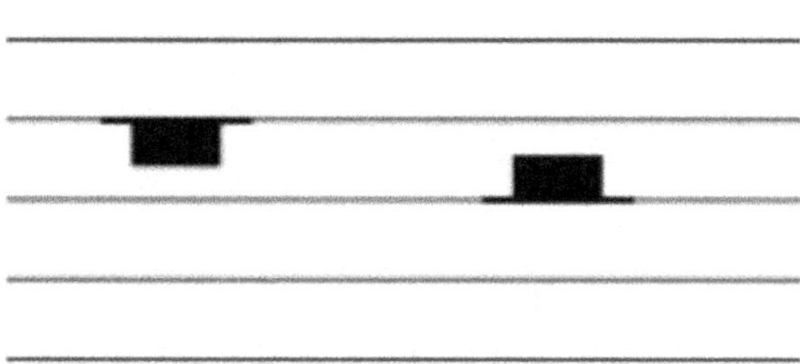

Whether it's facing up or down, that means it's a rest. Facing down, it's a whole rest, so four beats. Facing up, it's a half rest, or two beats.

These indicate shorter rests:

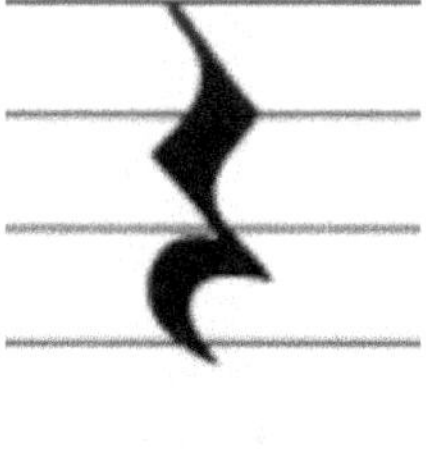

This is a quarter rest.

And this is an eighth rest. You count them just like you count the musical notes, but you don't play anything. These symbols stand for silence, and once again they indicate to you the rhythm of a piece.

Learning these basics of piano sheet music are helpful because while you can learn a song using guitar tabs for the guitar and ukulele, if you're ever unsure about the rhythm of a piece, you can look it up on sheet music and see how long each note is and figure out the rhthym.

Vocabulary

Here are some terms that you'll need to be familiar with, especially for piano, for when you pick up sheet music or if you are performing with others.

- Playing in Different Keys: This means that the position of your finger stays the same but the root note changes. For example, "I'm playing in F major instead of C major." Same chord position, but different notes, because you moved your fingers higher or lower on the guitar or piano.

- Arrangement: This is for if you're playing with a group. The arrangement decides who is playing what notes on the chord, which tempos, and when.
- Chord Extensions: This means adding alterations to a chord, which can make it sound completely different even if the basic notes are the same.
- Rhythm: This is how many pop songs can sound different even though they are all using the same chord. The rhythm is one of the first things that people notice when listening to a song, so changing it up can change the song almost completely.
- Melody: These are the varying notes that you play over the base chord—again, a way to take the same chord and make it sound different.
- Lyrics: You probably know this one already, but lyrics are the words that someone sings in time to the music.
- Adagio: This means to go slowly.
- Allegro: This means to play quickly.
- Beat: This is another word for rhythm.
- Leggiero: This is used mostly in piano, and means to play 'lightly' without putting too much force on the keys.
- Time Signature: How many beats are in each bar of music. So if there are eight beats, then the time signature is eight. The more beats, the faster you play.

- Bridge: A transitional passage. The repeated lyrics that a singer sings just before the chorus is the bridge—it literally 'bridges' the versus to the chorus.
- Chorus: The repeated phrase of the song, the heart of the song's meaning and music.
- Measure: One complete cycle of the time signature.
- Meter: This is the pattern of the rhythm. Think of it as the pauses in between the beats.
- Forte: To play strong and powerfully.
- Piano: This isn't the instrument—if someone says to play piano, it means to play it gently.
- Tempo: This is the overall speed of the piece. The meter and beat and rhythm make up the tempo.
- Rest Signs: This indicates when you stop playing your instrument and let it 'rest' for a period of time. This is usually done when you're playing with other instruments, so you all get your turn in the spotlight.
- Notes: The indication of what string or key you should be playing and for how long. Depending on the shape or shading of the note, it'll tell you how long to hold it for.

Chapter Three: The Seven Exercises

Now that you understand what your instruments are, how they work, how to read and understand music and bar chords, you're fully equipped to sally forth and play these instruments like a pro. Here are the seven basic exercises that will help you to play pretty much any song in the world.

Exercise One:

We're going to start with a C Major chord. This is the easiest chord to learn. Lots of songs, including "Are We Out of the Woods" by Taylor Swift and "Stay with Me" by Sam Smith use this key.

So, if you're on a guitar or ukulele, put your index finger on the first fret of the second string (B string). Then put your middle finger on the fourth string, on the second fret (this is the D string). Your ring finger goes on the third fret of the fifth string, or A string, and that's it! You don't play the sixth string, E, and the other two strings, e and G, are played open, so no fingers on those frets. Here's a picture of what that looks like on a guitar:

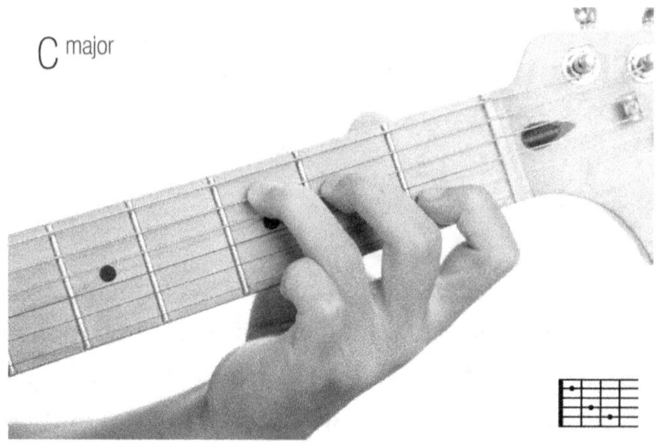

To play this on piano, you want to do these three keys that are in red:

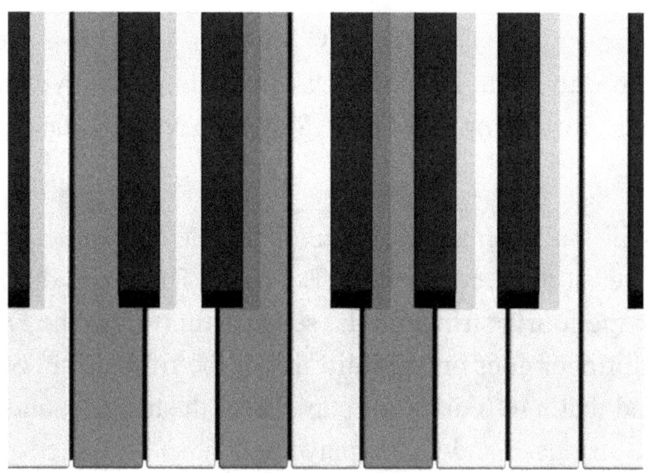

You can play them in any part of the piano, it's still the same chord. Practice doing it on the piano and on the guitar—remember to only strum five of the strings, not the E string—and on the ukulele, until you can do it in a steady rhythm of one, two, three, four.

To get an idea of how rhythm can completely change this song, do this chord while singing "Are We Out of the Woods" by Taylor Swift. You can play the song itself to accompany you if you feel more comfortable with that. Feel how fast that chord is. Then play "Stay with Me" by Sam Smith. This is very slow, with the chord playing, and then a long rest. That change in rhythm completely changes how the song feels.

Exercise Two:

Next exercise is the G major chord! "You Shook Me All Night Long" by AC/DC and "Heart of Gold" by Birdy are two G major chord songs, and again, very different in sound because of the rhythm.

Put your index finger on second fret of the fifth string, or A string. Then put your middle finger on the third fret of the bottom string, the E string. Your ring finger goes on the third fret of the e string, the first string, and your pinkie doesn't have to do anything. Keep in mind that your index and middle fingers have to be arched up so they don't accidentally brush other strings. This is where using your fingertips is important.

Here's an image of what your hand should look like:

Here is that same chord on the piano:

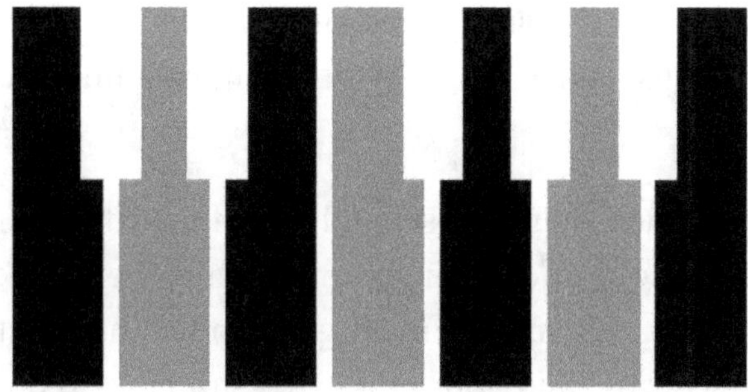

The red are the ones you want to be hitting. Use your
fingertips on your thumb, middle finger, and pinkie, so that you

don't hit any other keys while you're playing this. Again, practice just doing this on your guitar and piano and ukulele as just a one, two, three, four beat rhythm. Don't try to rush things. Try out the two songs, by Birdy and AC/DC, just to feel the difference the rhythm and the melody of the singer can do to change a song that has the same chords.

Exercise Three:

Next we're doing the D chord. This is an important chord on guitar for pop songs, so while you wouldn't normally learn it as quickly if you were studying piano for classical music, you're going to learn it here so that you can play all those songs on piano and guitar easily. Songs that use the D Major Chord include "Send My Love (to Your New Lover)" by Adele and "The Boys are Back in Town" by Thin Lizzy.

Put your index finger on the second fret of the fourth string, or G string. Then put your middle finger on the second fret of the sixth string, the e string, and then put your ring finger on the third fret of the fifth or B string.

If this chord seems a little more difficult for your fingers to handle on the guitar, that's how it should be. Some other very common chords that we're going to learn next are going to have four notes in them instead of just three, so this D major chord will help you, especially so that you can learn the F Major chord for the next exercise.

This is what this chord looks like on the guitar:

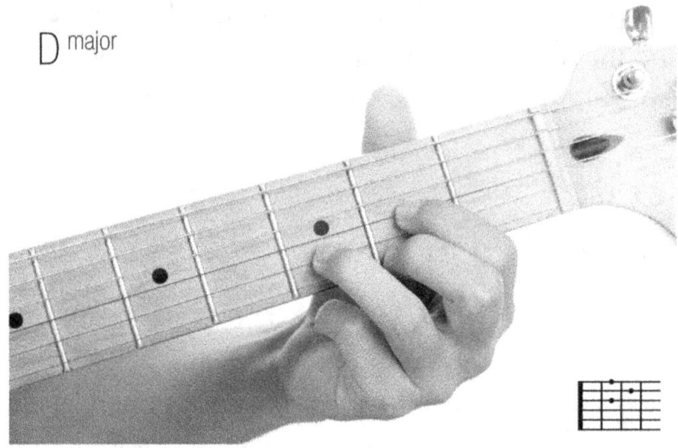

And this is what it looks like on piano:

Notice that for this you're using one black key on the piano. Practice strumming on guitar or ukulele and getting the rhythm on the piano, using the two songs as accompaniment to help you if you feel you need it. Having a song in mind as your goal can be helpful as it helps you to integrate the idea of a rhythm into your playing.

Exercise Four:

Now we're getting into that F Major Chord that we mentioned. "Still Into You" by Paramore, "What's My Age Again?" by Blink-182, and "Ain't No Rest for the Wicked" by Cage the Elephant are all in this key. It's a popular one.

This is the first chord that uses four fingers on the guitar, and it's difficult because it's a bar chord. This means you have to take your index finger and put it down across the first fret on all of the strings. Yup, all of them. This will take some getting used to because your finger needs to build up the strength to hold all six strings (or four strings, for the ukulele) down at the same time.

Keep in mind that your finger shouldn't be directly on the fret. Rather, it should be directly behind the fret. So when you put your finger on, say, the second fret of the D string, your fingertip should actually be right before the line of the fret. This actually gives you less work to do as the fret can then do its job to hold the string in place and help it resonate. If you ever pluck a guitar string and it doesn't have a clear, resonating sound, it's probably because your finger is on the fret rather than behind it.

So, put your index finger across all the strings on the first fret. Then put your middle finger on the second fret of the third or G string, your ring finger on the third fret of the fifth or A string, and your pinkie on the third fret of the fourth or D string. This is how it should look on guitar:

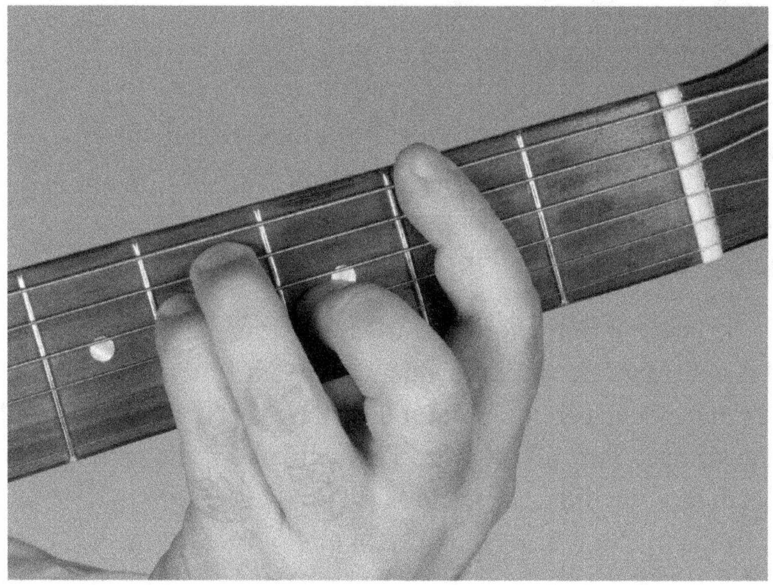

Notice how the index finger looks curved? You're going to have to do that in order to cover all of the frets while giving your other fingers the room to press on their strings.

On piano, however, this is one of the easiest chords. It looks like this:

You don't even have to stretch your fingers. Practice with this chord as well and get the feel for it.

Exercise Five:

We're going to get really fancy now. This exercise, you're going to practice doing a chord progression.

Songs progress from one chord to another, generally in four sets. So you'll have four sets of three or four notes that you repeat, over and over again. Take the F Major Chord that we just used. You won't keep your fingers on the same fret the entire song, but you will keep them in the same position. You just slide your hand up or down to hit different notes. Same with a piano. To play the full song, you keep your fingers in the same position and just move your and up or down the keyboard or neck of your guitar and ukulele.

For example, for "Ain't No Rest for the Wicked" by Cage the Elephant, you get your hands into the F major position. You start on the third fret. Then move your hand until the index finger is on the fifth fret. Now move it so your index finger is on the eighth fret. Now move your index finger to the first fret. Now back down to the third fret.

You've now just played the entirety of the song, all without moving your fingers, just sliding your hand up and down and strumming to the beat. Do that with all of the songs on guitar and piano and ukulele: find the notes on the sheet music and move your hands up and down until you've got it all down.

Exercise Six:

So, our next mission: practicing those chord progressions. Let's take a look at this handy dandy chart:

Common Chord Progressions to Practice:
I - IV - V
ii - V - I
I - V - IV - V
I - V - vi - IV
I - V - iii - IV
ii - IV - I - V
vi - ii - V - I
vi - iii - IV - I

See how you can look at the notes both on piano sheet music, on the charts, and on guitar tabs? Chord progressions are often written in roman numerals. So G major is I, and C major is IV.

The list of progressions at the bottom is what you need to practice. You switch your fingers from chord to chord. Start just with the four that you know. The I-V-vi-IV chord progression, or G-D-em-C, is one of the most common in pop music. The only difference is the rhythm and which one of these four you start on, but it's the same order. So if you start on C, the next three notes are G, D, and em, then back to C again. If you start on D, then it's em, C, and then G before back to D. If you just practice going through these four, going slowly, then you can find you're playing pretty much every pop song that you know.

What's a metronome, you ask? This handy-dandy little thing:

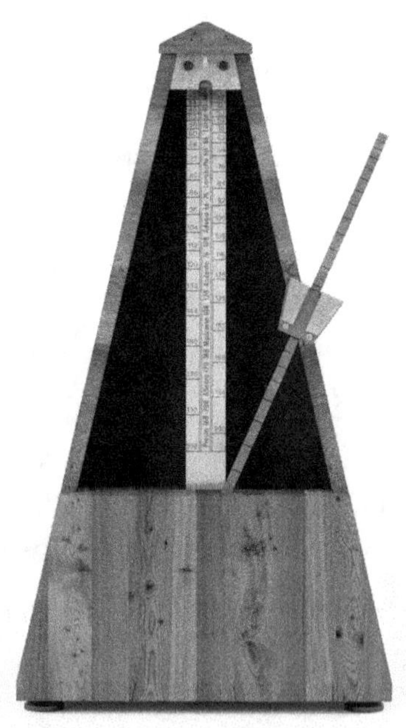

You can get a version on your phone or computer if you don't want to buy one. It keeps time for you. Put it on a slow setting and try to strum, or if you're on piano press down, in time with the metronome. This will help you improve your sense of rhythm while you do these chord progressions.

It's okay if you can't get all of these chord progressions right away. But by now your fingers will have gotten used to the positions on the piano and on the guitar, and you can always go back to the earlier exercises if you need. Just keep following these chord progressions until you're able to move back and forth smoothly between them.

Exercise Seven:

Here are some more chord progressions, this time in E major! What is E major for guitar and piano? It's a little more difficult, so here are some visuals:

You want your index finger on the fourth string on the first fret, your middle finger on the second string on the second fret, and your ring finger on the third string, also in the second fret—which is where it gets tricky, since you're having two fingers share that same space and need to press down on both strings in the same place. Your pinkie can stay out of the way. "Back in

Black" by AC/DC and "Pour Some Sugar on Me" by Def Leppard are two songs in the key of E Major.

Here's what it looks like on piano:

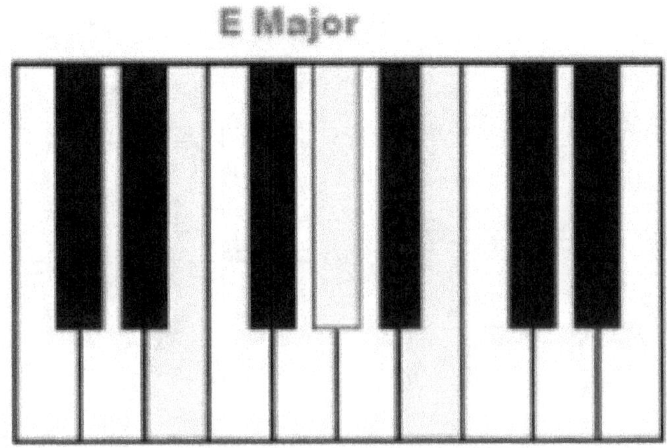

Again, much easier on piano than on guitar. You'll find that most of these chord progressions are easier to do on the piano rather than on guitar or ukulele, whereas reading sheet music for piano is harder than reading tabs and charts for guitar. It's a give and take, but both instruments are easily translatable into the other.

Here are the chord progressions for E Major:

Common Chord Progressions to Practice:
I - IV - V7
ii - V7 - I
I - V7 - IV - V
I - V7 - vi - IV
I - V7 - iii - IV
ii - IV - I - V7
vi - ii - V7 - I
vi - iii - IV - I

Look at it as a chart, as a tab, as sheet music, and as roman numerals. The more you practice, the more you'll be able to just look at any one of these and understand. Go through the chord progressions on this sheet, and the previous one, and you'll know pretty much everything there is to know about playing basic songs by the time that you're through.

It's almost unbelievable how easy it is to pick all of this up—constant practice is the key, but with these fundamentals, you'll be wowing your friends and family in no time. In the next chapter, we'll explore some tips to keep in mind not just as you do these exercises but as you progress further.

Chapter Four: Tips for Practicing

So now we're going to go over some random tips that'll help you out as you're practicing. Keep in mind that everyone learns just a little bit differently, so what might work for one person won't work for you. But these are all things to keep in mind as you practice the seven exercises:

Tip #1:

Practice doing your chord shapes one finger at a time, if you're having trouble remember where to keep all of your fingers. Starting with just one finger at a time can help take the pressure off and keep you from getting confused. There's no harm in starting slow.

Tip #2:

Practice the chord shapes without strumming. Again, no harm in starting slow if that's what you need. The key here is to get those chords memorized so that you can play any song that you want, so don't rush forward if you don't have those.

Tip #3:

Pay attention to the chord changes. Transitions are the hardest thing to get down, so you'll want to practice those a lot. It'll seem hard at first, switching the positions of your fingers, more so on guitar than on piano since you're bending your wrist into an odd shape. With piano, the struggle will be teaching your fingers how to stretch out. But don't get discouraged! Practice transitions.

Tip #4:

Keep your metronome slow. I know, you want to go fast! And you'll be surprised by how fast even the slower songs feel once you start playing them. Getting these exercises down is what matters, not the speed.

Tip #5:

Make a practice plan and stick to it. This can go both ways—don't overbook yourself, but don't sell yourself short, either. Plan for a good amount of time that works easily with your schedule. Otherwise you'll find yourself making excuses. Say, for example, you've planned to practice for an hour every day. But when you get home from work, you find that the idea of practicing for a whole hour is just too draining. So you make excuses to not do it, thinking you'll make up the time later. Or, conversely, say you've promised yourself that you'll practice for ten minutes a day—and then get frustrated when you're not making a lot of progress. Find a time that isn't too ambitious but still gives you a good solid bit to practice your exercises.

Tip #6:

Find a chord dictionary so that when you've progressed beyond the more basic chords of these songs you can learn new ones and keep in practice. It's amazing the amount of chords and chord variations that are out there, and once you've mastered these, you can get really fancy and wow everyone. This is especially true of piano—once you've mastered these exercises and chords, go ahead and get a beginner's piano book with some classical pieces in it. You'll be surprised at how many you'll be able to play!

Tip #7:

It's important to keep your fingers and wrists healthy.
Remember that with piano, your wrist is supposed to be
completely relaxed, and your fingertips have to do a lot of
stretching but remain light. With guitar and ukulele, your wrist
has to be strong and in position, and your fingertips have to be
strong to put the right amount of pressure on the strings. It can be
easy for you to hurt your fingers and wrists over time if you don't
do proper exercises. Take time to bend your wrists, rotate them,
clench and unclench your fist (a small exercise ball is good for
this) and practice lifting and extending your fingers and holding
the position. It might seem silly, but doing these exercises before
you play will help to prevent hand cramps and wrist pain later on.
Below is an example of some wrist exercises that you can to do
help keep your wrists flexible, strong, and healthy. A ten-minute
warm up for your fingers and wrists might very well seem silly,
but carpel tunnel syndrome and other health hazards have
seriously affected the performance of guitarists and pianists for
years, including famous ones. It's better to do some warming up
than to spend months in pain and unable to practice.

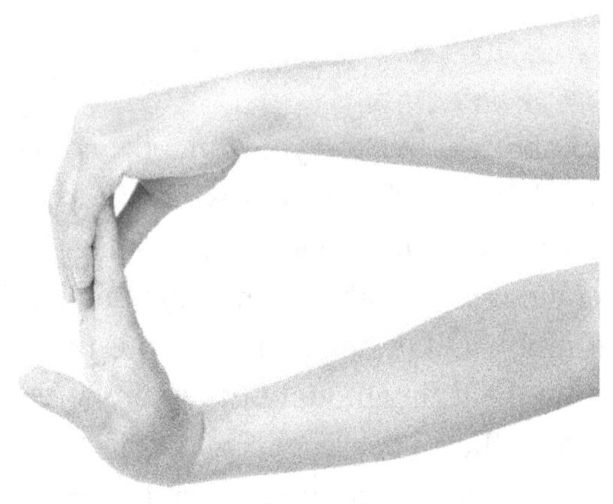

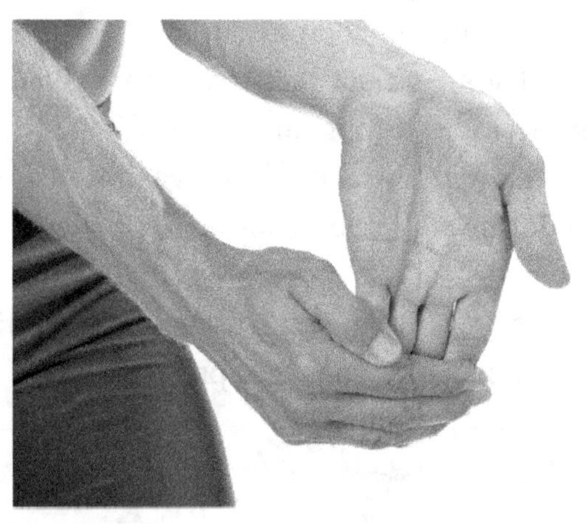

Tip #8:

If you find yourself getting frustrated or tired, or like you want to smash your piano to bits, then take a break. Walk away and get some fresh air. You won't learn if you find yourself hating practice, so go easy on yourself!

Tip #9:

Regular practice is better than how much you practice. Practicing for twenty minutes a day is better than practicing for two hours once a week. You want the repetition to get into your fingers.

Tip #10:

Count out loud as you practice your rhythms when you're doing these chords. It might sound silly, but it helps you to integrate the rhythm into your head. Some prefer, for example, to count using numbers. Others use phrases corresponding to the notes on the sheet music: "whole note hold it," for a whole note, or "quarter dot" for a quarter note with a dot on it. Whatever you use doesn't matter so long as you say it out loud to practice.

Tip #11:

Explore and have fun! Go onto the internet and find videos that show you how to play new songs. Go to a local jam session or open mike night at a café and perform for some people. Try writing your own songs or playing around with chord combinations. You learned these instruments because you wanted to, so don't lose sight of that. Do this for your own enjoyment.

Chapter Five: Moving Beyond the Basics

Ideas to keep in mind as you progress to more complicated chords, especially on the piano, and the idea of songwriting, and how these instruments can all play together at the same time.

Keep in mind chord changes and how they affect the song. You want your transitions to be smooth, for the sound to be clear and to resonate, and for you to get good at knowing where to place your fingers without having to pause and look.

Piano and guitar, and even ukulele, are great instruments for accompanying singers. You're going to get a lot of requests to accompany people when they want to sing a song, and you're probably going to want to sing a song yourself while providing your own accompaniment. As you gain confidence, you'll be tempted to really let your playing skills shine. Don't! The melody, and therefore the singer, is the star of the show. Practice playing at the right volume without too much energy so that you don't drown out the singer and steal the show, even if it's from yourself. After all, your chords are great but what if no one can hear what you're singing?

You're going to sometimes run into a problem where you have a piece on guitar tabs that you want to translate to piano sheet music, and vice versa. Doing this should wait until you've gotten comfortable with chord progressions and the exercises listed previously. You'll be able to figure out dozens of songs just by doing the chord progressions using different rhythms and accompanying a recording of a song (it can help to get an instrumental copy of said song, so the singer doesn't distract you with her melody). But when the time comes, here's a good example using the classic "Stairway to Heaven":

Tabs and sheet music are, fortunately, both on lines. So you would start by looking at what line the first note is on. It should say 7 and be on the third line from the bottom: the seventh fret of the D string. Now, you count backwards seven frets until you get to the open string—and count backwards on the piano at the same time. D, D#, E, F, F#, G, G#, and then ending on A. So the first note you'd play for this on the piano is A.

You just keep transcribing that way, counting backwards on the piano from how many frets there are on the guitar, to find each note. It's time consuming, but once you've moved past the beginning stages and want to learn more complicated songs like "Stairway to Heaven," you'll find yourself in this position a lot.

Piano can be especially difficult to learn as you progress further in your understanding of music. With the guitar, you'll want to start to simply incorporate the melody—this means plucking individual strings in between the strumming of the chords. But integrating the piano melody can take a lot of practice as you're moving both hands in different ways simultaneously. This is where fundamentals are important. Return to your chords when you feel frustrated and keep practicing those. Work on tapping each individual key out to improve your fingers' ability to move independently. And do the fundamentals like learn your scales. They're not necessary to learn for these chord songs, but if you want to move beyond that into more classical pieces, then you'll have to start learning them.

As you progress, you'll start to develop your own personal style. You might add a little flair to your version of "Don't Stop Believing" by Journey, or perhaps you moved your middle finger up to switch to a minor key for when you play "Hey, Jude" by the Beatles on the piano. That is totally right and natural to do. Embrace your personal style and as you grow in confidence, experiment. Experimenting on already-existing chords and chord songs is how new chord songs are made, so have at it.

If you want to start getting into songwriting, there are tons of ways that you can go about it. Tom Waits, a singer-songwriter, would play multiple radios at once to find where the songs overlapped in their chords. You might find that the chords of one song would match the riff of another, and combining them makes your own song.

Another way to do it is don't give yourself time to second-guess anything. Set a timer for fifteen minutes. You now have to get your song written in that time. Ready, set, go! This eliminates your ability to second-guess yourself and agonize over a particular chord. You never know what you'll find when you're racing against the clock.

And sometimes, just stop listening to music. Stare out the window for a while. Revel in the silence. Spend a day not talking, just listening to everything around you. Shutting off one of your sensory inputs or outputs, whether it's forcing yourself to just stare out of your skylight, promising yourself not to talk, or not listening to anything. Removing one sense can heighten the others and give your brain a chance to rest and see things in a new way that might give you the inspiration that you need.

If you've moved past the chord progressions and have learned the songs in this book and still want to go further, remember, you can always get yourself a teacher. Even if that 'teacher' is someone on the internet who posts videos about their work on ukulele or piano or whatnot, they can be a source of inspiration and added learning for you as you move farther along in your study of music. There's only so much that you can learn on your own without someone helping to walk you through the more complicated parts, so if you find yourself moving past the chord songs and want to challenge yourself, a teacher can be someone to help walk you through that.

Similarly to that, join in the conversation in the music world! Look up what musicians are saying about their work, listen to new songs, join a band, go listen to an open mike night. You can't operate in a vacuum and collaborating with others, even if that collaboration is just you sitting and listening, is an important part of the artistic process. Find a group of people that you can share ideas with and who you can learn from. You'd be surprised at how it helps improve not only your playing but your understanding of music in general.

Chapter Six: Chord Songs

Here is a list of different songs that you can play using the basic chords. Most of them use the most popular "pop music" chord that we previously discussed, but others use some of the six other chords. Now that you know the basic chords you can play any of these songs with ease—you just have to learn the tempo. One of my personal favorites, and the song that I started learning when I was a beginner, is "Ain't No Rest for the Wicked" by Cage the Elephant. If you're a little amazed by how many songs are on here, just think of how your friends will feel when you sit down at a piano or whip out your guitar or ukulele and find that you've turned into a musical genius. It's all in those basic chords.

Something to keep in mind is that the melody will vary from song to song. That's not actually what matters when playing the song, though. If you play the right chord, in the right rhythm, you'll actually be fine. In fact in a lot of bands, one guitar plays just the chords while the other plays the melody. If you have the chords down, the audience will know the song—especially if you're singing, because your voice then carries the melody so you don't have to worry about actually doing it with your guitar. Helpful, right?

I-V-vi-IV Songs:

The following songs are songs that are done using the most common chord, I-V-vi-IV. Many people have pointed out the use of this chord in pop songs, and while some would argue it's overused, this is good news for you because with this chord you can play hundreds of different songs using this one chord. Songs that use this chord include:

Don't Stop Believing by Journey

You're Beautiful by James Blunt

Forever Young by Alphaville

I'm Yours by Jason Mraz

Hey Soul Sister by Train

Wherever You Will Go by The Calling

Can You Feel the Love Tonight by Elton John (from The Lion King)

Take Me Home, Country Roads by John Denver

She Will Be Loved by Maroon Five

Let it Be by The Beatles

When I Come Around by Green Day

Save Tonight by Eagle Eye Cherry

Africa by Toto

Behind These Hazel Eyes by Kelly Clarkson

One of Us by Joan Osborne

Complicated by Avril Lavigne

Apologize by OneRepublic

Otherside by Red Hot Chili Peppers

Kids by MGMT

Superman by Five for Fighting

Going by Key:

Another way that you can look up songs is to look them up by the major chord. The following are songs divided by the chords that we learned in our exercises.

C Major Songs:

Happier by Ed Sheeran

Heaven by Bryan Adams

How Does it Feel by Avril Lavigne

Sweetest Devotion by Adele

When My Heart Beats Like a Hammer by B.B. King

Bang Bang by Ariana Grande

Stay with Me by Sam Smith

Are We Out of the Woods by Taylor Swift

Minority by Green Day

Stockholm Syndrome by Muse

Use Somebody by Kings of Leon

Wanted (Dead or Alive) by Bon Jovi

Stay by Rihanna featuring Mikky Echo

G Major Songs:

Under the Tide by Chvrches

Make You Feel Better by Red Hot Chili Peppers

Wake by Linkin Park

You Shook Me All Night Long by AC/DC

How Do We (Party) by Rita Ora

Shake it Off by Taylor Swift

Welcome to New York by Taylor Swift

Heart of Gold by Birdy

Been a Son by Nirvana

Whiskey in the Jar by Thin Lizzy

She's a Rebel by Green Day

Here I Go Again by White Snake

Little Wing by Jimi Hendrix

Sweet Home Alabama by Lynyrd Skynyrd

Wonderful Tonight by Eric Clapton

Call Me Maybe by Carly Rae Jepsen

I Gotta Feeling by The Black-Eyed Peas

Swing Swing by All-American Rejects

Good Riddance (Time of Your Life) by Green Day

Wake Me Up When September Ends by Green Day

D Major Songs:

Send My Love (To Your New Lover) by Adele

We Sink by Chvrches

Castle on the Hill by Ed Sheeran

Align by Nina Nesbitt

All is Now Harmed by Ben Howard

Lithium by Nirvana

Settle Down by The 1975

Home by Gabrielle Aplin

Grow Up by Paramore

Wake Up by Rage Against the Machine

Hysteria by Muse

Under the Bridge by Red Hot Chili Peppers

Times Like These by The Foo Fighters

Only Girl (In the World) by Rihanna

Love Story by Taylor Swift

Summer of '69 by Bryan Adams

Hey There Delilah by The Plain White T

E Major Songs:

Break My Heart by Hey Violet

Don't Tell Me by Avril Lavigne

All I Ask by Adele

Piano by Ariana Grande

Ain't it Fun by Paramore

Basket Case by Green Day

Buck Rogers by Feeder

Back in Black by AC/DC

Sex on Fire by Kings of Leon

Pour Some Sugar on Me by Def Leppard

Midnight Memories by One Direction

Fat Lip by Sum 41

I Believe in a Thing Called Love by The Darkness

F Major Songs:

Ain't No Rest for the Wicked by Cage the Elephant

I'm Not the Only One by Sam Smith

Blank Space by Taylor Swift

What's My Age Again by Blink-182

Party in the U.S.A. by Miley Cyrus

Still into You by Paramore

The Wind Cries Mary by Jimi Hendrix

The House of the Rising Sun by The Animals

Bed of Roses by Bon Jovi

Scar Tissue by Red Hot Chili Peppers

Just the Way You Are by Bruno Mars